T0284004

Insights You Need from
Harvard
Business
Review

SUPPLY CHAIN

Insights You Need from Harvard Business Review

Business is changing. Will you adapt or be left behind?

Get up to speed and deepen your understanding of the topics that are shaping your company's future with the **Insights You Need from Harvard Business Review** series. Featuring HBR's smartest thinking on fast-moving issues—blockchain, cybersecurity, AI, and more—each book provides the foundation introduction and practical case studies your organization needs to compete today and collects the best research, interviews, and analysis to get it ready for tomorrow.

You can't afford to ignore how these issues will transform the landscape of business and society. The Insights You Need series will help you grasp these critical ideas—and prepare you and your company for the future.

Books in the series include:

SUPPLY CHAIN

Harvard Business Review Press
Boston, Massachusetts

Copyright 2023 Harvard Business School Publishing Corporation

All rights reserved
Printed in the United States of America

10 9 8 7 6 5 4 3 2 1

No part of this publication may be reproduced, stored in or introduced into a retrieval system, or transmitted, in any form, or by any means (electronic, mechanical, photocopying, recording, or otherwise), without the prior permission of the publisher. Requests for permission should be directed to permissions@harvardbusiness.org, or mailed to Permissions, Harvard Business School Publishing, 60 Harvard Way, Boston, Massachusetts 02163.

The web addresses referenced in this book were live and correct at the time of the book's publication but may be subject to change.

Library of Congress Cataloging-in-Publication Data

Names: Harvard Business Review Press, issuing body.
Title: Supply chain / Harvard Business Review.
Other titles: Supply chain (Harvard Business Review Press) | Insights you need from Harvard Business Review.
Description: Boston, Massachusetts : Harvard Business Review Press, [2023] | Series: The insights you need from Harvard Business Review | Includes index.
Identifiers: LCCN 2023017384 (print) | LCCN 2023017385 (ebook) | ISBN 9781647825966 (paperback) | ISBN 9781647825973 (epub)
Subjects: LCSH: Business logistics. | Industrial management. | Success in business.
Classification: LCC HD38.5 .S874 2023 (print) | LCC HD38.5 (ebook) | DDC 658.5—dc23/eng/20230531
LC record available at https://lccn.loc.gov/2023017384
LC ebook record available at https://lccn.loc.gov/2023017385

ISBN: 978-1-64782-596-6
eISBN: 978-1-64782-597-3

The paper used in this publication meets the requirements of the American National Standard for Permanence of Paper for Publications and Documents in Libraries and Archives Z39.48-1992.

Contents

Contents

Section 3

Innovation in Your Supply Chain

Section 4

Navigating Supplier Relationships

Contents

Section 5
Implementing Sustainable Practices

Introduction

SUPPLY CHAIN RESILIENCY IN A CHANGING WORLD

by Willy C. Shih

In its simplest form, the goal of supply chain management is to efficiently match the supply of products and services with the demand of end customers. Historically the focus has been on sourcing: managing the flow of materials and resources as they move through value-adding stages until they become finished products and services to the point of delivery to customers. Over the last few decades, supply chains have evolved to become global, efficiently delivering a cornucopia of products to consumers around the world. And the environment has been benign, with steadily falling trade barriers and increased global integration.

A series of historic shocks have put both the structure and the fragility of global supply chains top of mind for leaders everywhere. The Covid-19 pandemic, geopolitics, the war in Ukraine, climate change, and other global societal challenges have wreaked havoc upon companies, disrupting supplies, causing rapid shifts in demand, and exposing vulnerabilities and unexpected constraints. The shifts led to bottlenecks in production and logistics networks and widespread shortages in everything from toilet paper and cleaning supplies to bicycles and freezers. Shortages of semiconductors forced automakers to park partially completed vehicles in fields, while the U.S.–China trade war and tariffs led to the shifting of production of many goods to Southeast Asia, India, Mexico, and elsewhere. Companies found themselves unable to meet the needs of customers, sometimes for months on end. Or after the initial crunch, aggressive stockpiling left some with *excess* inventory they were unable to sell. Neither case has been good, costing companies money and customer satisfaction. And the feeling of uncertainty and frustration continues.

The malfunctioning of supply chains made headlines around the world, and their robustness and reliable functioning has moved from a core operations responsibility to a topic of boardroom and government discussions everywhere. Now is the time to revisit the design assumptions underpinning global supply chains and consider how some of those might change in a rapidly evolving geopolitical environment.

Understanding all the links and the relationships with suppliers will take on added importance in the dynamic environment we face today. A new awareness of the environmental impact of transporting goods over long distances, or labor and business practices of distant suppliers will motivate leaders and managers alike to consider how this affects consumer perception of their brands, products, and services. And taking a step back and considering the broad range of issues that affect supply chain design and implementation will better prepare them for a future that will demand more agility, resiliency, and adaptability in responding to customer needs.

Supply Chain: The Insights You Need from Harvard Business Review seeks to help leaders and managers get up to speed on the rapidly evolving research and thinking around supply chains, and discover ways to make them more resilient without sacrificing competitive advantage in a highly dynamic environment. It does this in five sections.

The first section focuses on building resilience. Though the crises of the last few years were caused by widespread and sudden shifts in supply-and-demand patterns, they are not likely to be the last disruptions the world sees. In chapter 1, Christian Schuh, Wolfgang Schnellbächer, and Daniel Weise, coauthors of *Profit from the Source*, argue that many so-called unforeseen events *can* be predicted. They discuss how companies can sense and monitor these risks to help them be better prepared for the next crisis. Chapter 2 explains why it's so difficult to map your supply chain, especially when it has grown into an interconnected global network. This chapter helps you to better see and understand that network—and your place in it. Next, you'll learn how to be more strategic, rather than reactive, in the face of disruption. Inventory shortfalls during the pandemic caused many people to question just-in-time (JIT) practices and lean supply chains, but professors Man-Mohan Sodhi and Thomas Choi suggest embracing a modified form of JIT that builds in buffers. The section closes with a look at small and midsized suppliers and how investing in new technology makes the entire supply chain more productive, sustainable, and resilient.

Section 2 shifts to looking at a debate in the supply chain world: regionalization versus globalization. Just as supply chains have grown more interconnected, over the last three decades they have also become increasingly global in extant, driven by a dramatic expansion of the tradable sector. Many firms have shifted to a global sourcing model, allowing them to take advantage of lower labor and materials costs, land, and other costs. But in the face of disruption, some companies have brought the production of key components and inventory closer to home. Suketu Gandhi, cohead of the global Strategic Operations Practice at Kearney, explains how new technologies like AI, 3D printing, and digital manufacturing solutions can help companies reshape their supply chains to serve what customers really value while relocating production nearby. But research scholars Steven Altman and Caroline Bastian take a skeptical view on this approach and question whether short-distance, close-to-market production will substantially displace long-distance trade. In chapter 6, they caution managers to factor geopolitical tensions into their thinking before jumping into regional options. While the debate over regionalization is ongoing, the outcome will have significant implications for trade patterns, jobs, and the development of emerging economies.

In section 3, we turn our attention to unique innovations in supply chain management. Over the course of the pandemic, the bullwhip effect, where demand variability increases as one goes upstream in a supply chain, was a major cause of supply-demand imbalances across numerous product sectors. To combat this, chapter 7 suggests stepping away from traditional forecasting approaches and introduces a new methodology called flow-casting, which starts with retail sales to end users and then moves upstream to calculate demand and inventory flows. Additionally, chapter 8 explores how digitizing a supply chain and building a digital platform can enable companies to bring in new partners and generate new opportunities, using Haier's COSMOPlat platform as an example. By tying together partners in an ecosystem, they can collaborate with cooperative innovation and design, enabling their value chains to evolve with changing times.

We'd be remiss in this book if we didn't discuss an essential element in supply chain: suppliers. In chapter 9, I urge firms to consider the health of their suppliers by moving beyond transactional deals to treating them as strategic partners. Next, Maria Jesús Saénz, Elena Revilla, and Inma Borrella look at how digital technology and platforms are changing the nature of supplier relationships, and how managers can take on a boundary-spanning mindset to enhance agility, flexibility, collaboration, experimentation, and trust. Section 4 ends with a unique look at how artificial intelligence–powered software—a chatbot—helps Walmart to automate procurement negotiations. Out of 89 suppliers, the chatbot was successful in reaching an agreement with 64% of them with an average negotiation turnaround of only 11 days.

The final section features articles on taking sustainable action. Labor practices and the sustainable use of resources are increasingly important issues for leaders and managers as companies face increasing scrutiny from advocacy groups, financial analysts, the media, and customers. Chapter 12 provides an approach to simplifying the currently complex system of audits in the apparel industry and calls for use of more independent third parties who can employ standardized audit frameworks. And in the book's final chapter, professors Verónica Villena and Dennis Gioia address some of the challenges in cascading sustainability goals down through multitiered supply chains, highlighting how collaborative approaches can make sustainability initiatives more feasible. After all, as Villena and Gioia note, "A supply chain is only as strong as its weakest link."

As you read this book, it's not enough to simply understand the concepts but to use them in your daily work and strategy. Ask yourself these questions as you think about how to apply the themes and ideas scattered throughout these pages to your own business:

- As the global trading environment continues to shift, where are the biggest risks for disruption in my company's supply chain? Where are potential new opportunities?

- Where can we build more resilient measures into the organization's supply chain operation? Do we have room to change or adapt quickly if necessary, and do we know what options are available to us?

- Has my organization reviewed our supplier relationships and how we manage them? Which are the truly strategic ones, and which expose us to disruption as well as ESG risks? How can we work with suppliers in more productive and more beneficial ways?

- How can new digital tools help us not only with visibility, but also with innovation? Which tools would be most helpful to our business? Where can we experiment with them?

The world has changed. While most leaders and managers grew up in a relatively benign world of expanding access to global production sources and markets, the future promises to be much more dynamic. Those who understand supply chain foundations as well as the best thinking on agility, resiliency, and some of the changing pressures will be better prepared for the more constrained and less certain world ahead.

Section 1

BUILDING RESILIENCE

1

THREE STEPS TO PREPARE YOUR SUPPLY CHAIN FOR THE NEXT CRISIS

by Christian Schuh, Wolfgang Schnellbächer, and Daniel Weise

N o one can say they weren't aware of the possibility of a global pandemic or of the numerous border disputes around the world causing increased volatility. Conflicts resulting from heightened geopolitical tensions could easily unbalance the entire semiconductor industry, but such disasters can be partially mitigated with sufficient risk monitoring.

Indeed, most of the risks that a company will face do not fall into the category of what the mathematician and philosopher Nassim Nicholas Taleb termed "black swan" events: random, highly improbable events that have enormous impact. A trade dispute, a viral epidemic, a product failure, a cybersecurity breach, a tsunami—these are not black swans but, as the business writer Michele Wucker memorably puts it, "gray rhinos": highly probable, highly predictable, high impact, but neglected threats that are charging toward the company like a crash of rhinos (who show visible signs of aggression and whose attacks can thus be predicted nearly 100% of the time).

In other words, they are "when," not "if," events—and this means they can be prepared for.

For many CEOs, preparing for something that may not happen on their watch will seem like a luxury they can ill afford. But, in fact, the benefits of doing so are not just about protecting on the downside. CEOs building resilient companies can expect to profit on the upside too:

- Companies that are well prepared and as a result prosper in a crisis can expect to recover more quickly than their competitors. In a review of corporate performance during the past four U.S. downturns (since 1985), Boston Consulting Group

(BCG) found that 14% of companies *increased* their sales and their profit margin.[1]

- Investors are starting to reward companies that build for the future by becoming more innovative and more resilient. In June 2020, during the depths of the Covid-19 pandemic, BCG surveyed major institutional investors and found that nine out of 10 believed it was "important for healthy companies to prioritize the building of business capabilities—even if it means lowering earnings-per-share guidance or delivering below consensus."[2]

So, CEOs have every reason to prepare for the next crisis—and no reason not to. But how, exactly, should they do it? They need to start building long-term resilience now. If they wait until the next crisis strikes, it will be too late. We recommend three steps.

Create a world-class sensing and risk-monitoring operation

To get a clear view of the likely risks in their supply chain, CEOs need to invest in risk intelligence and strategic foresight, creating a team of procurement superforecasters equipped with the latest artificial intelligence (AI)–powered sensing technology.[3] Effective risk-monitoring operations should encompass not only direct (or Tier 1) suppliers but also indirect (or Tier N) suppliers who operate deep within the supply chain. Also, it should take account of eight essential risk categories:

- Four associated with individual suppliers: operational, financial, reputational, and structural risks

- Three associated with a supplier's country or region: disasters, geopolitical, and fiscal risks

- One associated with a supplier's industry: industry risks

Within each of these categories, there are three or four specific risks. For example, a supplier's structural risk might be its dependence on one or two Tier 3 suppliers or its involvement in a hostile-takeover bid. A supplier's geopolitical risk might be its operations in a war zone or a territory that imposes tariffs and other trade barriers. And a supplier's industry risk might be its dependence on one or two monopolistic suppliers who then suffer a production delay.

Having established a framework, CEOs need to feed it with data linked to specific key risk indicators (KRIs). For example, operational KRIs might be the age of a supplier's machinery or the percentage of employees in workers' unions; industry KRIs might be the concentration of suppliers that could lead to bottlenecks, or a supplier's R&D into innovative technology and the likelihood of obsolescence; while disaster-risk KRIs might be the number of people vaccinated in the country and at the supplier or the number of power outages suffered by the company.

With this data, and with the help of an AI-powered algorithm, the specific risk can be plotted on a two-by-two matrix, with the Y axis reflecting the detectability of the risk and the X axis reflecting the impact of the risk (see figure 1-1). The four quadrants of the matrix correspond to:

- **Limited risk:** Hard-to-detect events that have a noncritical impact. If a risk is deemed to be limited, then it can be deprioritized and occasionally reviewed for any increased detectability.

- **Manageable risk:** Easy-to-detect events that have a noncritical impact. If a risk is found to be manageable, then it can be subject to automated tracking and daily review.

- **Disruptive risk:** Hard-to-detect events that have a critical impact. In this case, a company must establish

FIGURE 1-1

Risk matrix

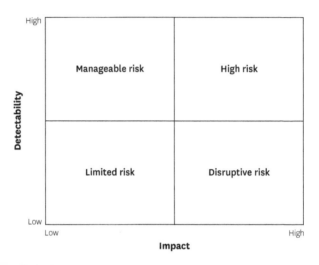

its likely probability, hedge proactively, simulate any possible negative impact, and prepare a reaction plan.

- **High risk:** Easy-to-detect events that have a critical impact. Here, a company must actively monitor the situation and take urgent steps to reduce the risk.

Once assessing where the risk falls on the matrix, companies are in a good position to determine what they need to do next.

Simplify your product portfolio

In the past few years, it has been the goal of companies to give consumers what they, as individuals, really want. Niche, highly personalized, "segment of one" products and services have become the norm. The trouble is that many of these products are low margin, lack a strategic purpose, require a broader range of suppliers, and lead to higher manufacturing, freight, and out-of-stock costs.

For these reasons, CEOs should look to scale back their product portfolios. That means eliminating some product lines and modifying the remaining products by simplifying their design, harmonizing their specifications, and standardizing their constituent raw materials, components, and other ingredients, as well as their packaging materials.

De-risk your supply chain

CEOs need to consider a series of risk-mitigation actions that encompass the three elements of the supply chain: sourcing the raw materials, components, and other parts of products; manufacturing the products; and delivering the parts to the factories and the products to the customers.

Take manufacturing, for example. CEOs should review their make-or-buy strategy, consider investing in digital technologies such as 3D printing, and above all, switch manufacturing to locations at home (reshoring), closer to home (near-shoring), or closer to consumer markets (regionalization).

The fast-fashion industry has long valued local manufacturing—primarily for speed. It now enjoys the additional benefits of lower supply chain risk. Similarly, Unilever has invested in highly mobile "nanofactories" housed in 40-foot shipping containers that can be sited pretty much anywhere, as need dictates.

CEOs should also consider taking back control of their supplies of critical raw materials and components. They can do this in a couple of ways.

During the last semiconductor shortage, we helped the CEO of a U.S. technology company prepare for the next (that is, the current) shortage by encouraging him to have his company develop contractual relationships with companies that are instrumental in every stage of the semiconductor supply chain— and with which they previously had no direct relationship. These include semiconductor vendors (such as Infineon and NXP), foundries (such as Taiwan Semiconductor Manufacturing Corporation [TSMC] and GlobalFoundries), integrated-circuit makers (such as

JCET and Amkor), and distributors (such as Avnet and Arrow Electronics).

Another way to take back control is to take ownership of vital components. This is what Tesla has done by designing and making its own microchips.

. . .

As CEOs tackle today's crises, it might seem perverse to have to start preparing for the next one. But it is essential that they do so. By taking the steps we've outlined, CEOs will ensure that their companies are well positioned for the rebound in the post-crisis phase.

TAKEAWAYS

Most risks that a company will face are not random, highly improbable black swan events. In fact, most can be predicted and prepared for. Doing so entails taking three steps:

✓ Create a world-class sensing and risk-monitoring operation. Look into essential risk categories (including supplier, regional, and industry risks) and assess how likely a risk is to occur.

✓ **Simplify your product portfolio.** Don't rely too much on highly personalized or niche "segment of one" products and services. Instead, eliminate some product lines and modify the remaining ones by simplifying design, harmonizing specifications, and standardizing their components.

✓ **De-risk your supply chain.** Consider making changes in three areas of the supply chain: sourcing raw materials and components; manufacturing products; and delivering parts to the factories and the products to the customers.

NOTES

1. Martin Reeves et al., "Advantage in Adversity: Winning the Next Downturn," *BCG Henderson Institute Newsletter*, February 4, 2019, https://www.bcg.com/publications/2019/advantage-in -adversity-winning-next-downturn.

2. Hady Farag et al., "ESG Commitments Are Here to Stay," BCG, June 23, 2020, https://www.bcg.com/publications/2020/esg -commitments-are-here-to-stay.

3. Martin Högel et al., "Delivering on Digital Procurement's Promise," BCG, June 1, 2018, https://www.bcg.com/publications /2018/delivering-digital-procurement-promise.

Adapted from content posted on hbr.org, November 9, 2022 (product #H07CK2).

2

WHY IT'S SO HARD TO MAP GLOBAL SUPPLY CHAINS

by Vishal Gaur, Nikolay Osadchiy, and Maximiliano Udenio

The semiconductor chip shortage that hit the automotive industry in late 2020 highlighted two lessons in supply chain management.

The first is the lack of upstream visibility that remains the Achilles heel of supply chains. Firms often do not know their suppliers beyond those in Tier 1 and are thus prone to shocks in the upstream supply chain.

The second is that the supply chain of each firm is not isolated but is connected with other supply chains in a vast global network. This reality was made painfully apparent by the continuing shortages of semiconductors, when companies in different industries (for example, automotive and consumer electronics) found themselves vying for chips from the same suppliers.

The solution to these problems requires not only gaining visibility into the upper tiers of a firm's supply chain but also assessing which suppliers are prone to greater risk from the rest of global network.

Our 2021 study of this problem, "Have Supply Networks Become More Fragmented Over Time?" used a large public data set of supply linkages in the economy compiled by FactSet Revere. It enabled us to map more than 690,000 supply chain links across 47,390 firms in the global economy from 2003 to 2017. Although the data set is at the firm level and does not capture specific product-level linkages, our study revealed lessons. In this article, we illustrate our key insights with an example of the supply chains from five major chip manufacturers to seven major automobile manufacturers. (The seven include the combined Fiat and Chrysler, which merged in 2014.)

Supply chains are webs or networks

We found that supply chains are vast, dense, and dynamic. Between the five chipmakers and the seven automakers, there is an average of 90.5 intermediary firms each year. The average number of links that have to be traversed to go from a chipmaker to an automaker is 3.2. Moreover, there are multiple shortest paths from a single chipmaker to a single automaker in the same year (average = 7.9), and the majority of these links sit in different industries.

This supply network also keeps changing over time: A large number of links get disconnected and new links get formed each year. For example, there are only 14 intermediary firms that are common across the years of 2003 and 2017. Altogether, the collective network from 2003 to 2017 contains an astounding 416 intermediaries, 11,533 links, and 3,589 source-destination links.

Gaining supply chain visibility in such a complex network is an enormously difficult undertaking. In fact, it is not practical for any single firm to unilaterally take on the mantle of exploring its complete upstream supply chain. If the most downstream firm works backward, it would need a long time and considerable resources to explore its network tier by tier. Moreover, the dynamic structure of the supply network means that firms have to keep updating their knowledge of supply chains and reassessing their risks continuously.

Each firm's supply chain is interconnected with the global supply network

Semiconductor manufacturers supply chips to firms in a large number of industries. Indeed, we found that although the automotive industry is large, the seven carmakers in our example collectively made up less than 5% of the pathways originating from semiconductor chip manufacturers. The remaining 95% of the pathways led to firms in other industries such as computer manufacturing and consumer electronics. Similarly, the automotive manufacturers source not only chips but also many other components, so that the semiconductor supply chain is a small part of their own vast supply chains.

This phenomenon increasingly characterizes supply chains of companies. As products have become more complex over time, they require components from an expanding set of new suppliers. As a result, supply chains have become more interconnected, making firms susceptible to shocks that originate in other industries. The effects of such shocks have long been studied in the academic literature on capacity-constrained supply chains. If demand suddenly increases or decreases in another industry, then it can affect the ability of suppliers to fulfill orders in one's own industry. Particularly, in times of scarcity, these companies compete for valuable chips and components that use those chips.

Despite these changes, too often firms are focused on managing their buyer-supplier relationships as if they existed in isolation, ignoring the other firms that are connected with the same suppliers or the same buyers. Fortunately, the structure of the global supply network presents a solution to this problem.

The global supply network is fragmented into communities of firms

Using community-detection methods from the computer science literature, we found that the global supply network consists of communities or clusters. We discovered that there were dense supply chain linkages among firms inside each community and different communities were loosely connected with each other.

In this network, all suppliers are not equal sources of risk. There are some that assume greater importance because they sit at the boundaries of communities, meaning that they are gateways across communities and a disproportionate number of pathways pass through them. Such firms are called "high-betweenness firms." Our analysis of the global network identified these firms, and they are remarkably stable over time. Typically, these suppliers are distributors or manufacturers that have diverse industry representation among their customers.

This structure suggests a two-pronged approach. In the longer term, a firm—either on its own or, as we suggested is more practical, in collaboration with its Tier 1 suppliers—might establish a system for continuously mapping its supply chain. But in the shorter term, it might want to begin by trying to work with high-betweenness suppliers to gain information about its network. In fact, this strategy has become more relevant over time as the supply network has become more and more fragmented into loosely connected communities over the past two decades.

The effects of the Covid-19 pandemic, the subprime mortgage crisis, and other disruptions have shown how critically important it is to ensure the health of supply chains. Our study shows that firms, when managing their supply chains, need to keep in mind their connections with the larger network.

Supply chain disruptions have generated many recommendations for companies to map their supply chains, identify sources of the costliest risks, and take steps to mitigate them. But doing so is extremely challenging.

✓ Global supply chains are webs or networks, rather than straight lines. These networks are vast, dense, and dynamic.

✓ As products have become more complex, they require components from an expanding set of new suppliers. As a result, supply chains have become more interconnected.

✓ The global supply network consists of communities or clusters. Some suppliers assume greater importance because they sit at the boundaries of communities and are therefore more stable than others.

✓ Companies must think both long term and short term when considering how to work—and who to work with—in its supply chain.

Adapted from content posted on hbr.org, October 31, 2022 (product #H07B8E).

3

DON'T ABANDON YOUR JUST-IN-TIME SUPPLY CHAIN—REVAMP IT

by ManMohan S. Sodhi and Thomas Y. Choi

When Toyota initially created the just-in-time (JIT) approach to inventories, its factories and those of its suppliers were located near each other. Their proximity eliminated "wastes" like transit time and excessive inventory and enhanced collaboration at all levels.

Over the decades, companies extended the JIT concept to global supply chains. Still, the system continued to work, thanks to stable trade conditions and logistics capabilities worldwide, which made the delivery of items highly dependable and predictable. Now, turbulence and uncertainty have called into question the wisdom of continuing to operate factories on a just-in-time basis that are dependent on global supply chains.

These disruptions are tempting companies to throw out JIT and revert to "just-in-case" systems that maintain lots of inventory at various locations in the global supply chain to ensure business continuity. That would be a mistake. JIT remains the most efficient production system. Especially with interest rates rising, throwing it out and adding inventory haphazardly would mean hurting performance without necessarily improving resilience. A better option is to embrace a modified form of JIT—something that companies such as Toyota and Volkswagen are doing. It entails creating stockpiles or manufacturing capacity to protect your operation from supply chain disruptions.

Toyota adopted this approach after the 2011 earthquake in Japan's Fukushima Prefecture. It identified 500 priority parts, including semiconductor chips, whose lead times were very long and, therefore, vulnerable to disruptions. It then built a business-continuity plan requiring its suppliers to stockpile anywhere from two to six months' worth of semiconductor chips, depending on the lead time. As a result, in the spring of 2021, Toyota did not experience any shutdown or slowdowns, while rivals such as Volkswagen, General Motors, Ford, Honda, and Stellantis suffered. Any amount of buffer inventory, however, is still finite, and due to the prolonged chips shortage, Toyota eventually was affected and had to suspend production in some plants a year later.

Batteries for electric vehicles provide another example. As automakers increasingly switch to electric vehicles, they could rely on some of the world's largest lithium-ion battery manufacturers like LG Chem, Contemporary Amperex Technology, BYD, and Panasonic to deliver batteries just in time. However, with demand for electric vehicles expected to grow rapidly, manufacturers are not sure they can get supplies from these manufacturers on a regular JIT basis—or indeed at all. Consequently, Volkswagen is building buffers for its JIT plants globally, not by planning stockpiles of inventory of batteries but by building battery factories worldwide to ensure timely and continual supply.

How to Redesign a JIT Network

Companies can revamp their JIT supply chains by identifying their contiguous parts that can be run on a just-in-time basis and then connecting these "JIT supply chain segments" via buffers. These buffers need not just be stockpiles of inventory; they could also be excess or flexible capacity, or even resources such as warehouses or transportation shared with competitors and other companies. Thus, the company's supply chain becomes a network of linked JIT segments connected by buffers. Creating such a JIT network requires four steps.

1. Map your supply chain

While all companies know who their immediate suppliers are, many don't know their lower-tier suppliers, and delays or disruptions in the supply chain may come from these unknown suppliers' suppliers or even further upstream in the supply chain. The remedy is to map your supply chain extensively. Knowing who and where these suppliers are can help a company decide what parts or raw materials are the most vulnerable. Such a move paid off early in the pandemic for the minority of companies that had already done it, including Toyota, Western Digital, Micron Technology, and IBM.

2. Identify the segments that can be run on a JIT basis

The requisite conditions for a JIT segment include minimum fluctuations in demand, matching manufacturing cycle times across the nodes in the segment, and proximity of these nodes, which makes short transit times and close collaboration possible at various levels of the companies in the segment. Some segments may consist of just a single plant, while others may encompass suppliers across two or more tiers.

3. Create buffers at the points where the segments meet

Again, these buffers can comprise some combination of inventory, spare or backup capacity, redundant suppliers, and even facilities shared with other companies, including competitors. The differences in the production cycles of upstream and immediately downstream segments should determine the size of the buffer, whether it's inventory or production capacity.

One idea to enhance cost effectiveness is to use a single buffer to service two different JIT segments that face very different risks upstream. If one product line is vulnerable to geopolitical risk and another to natural disasters, both would be better off with a single buffer (rather than two separate ones). This buffer would cushion the downstream JIT segments of these product lines from any disruptions in their respective upstream sources. Such a buffer could be a warehouse with a stockpile of components for either line or a single flexible plant that can make the components.

Another idea is to ensure that different product lines in adjacent JIT segments have as many common parts as possible and create a buffer for these parts, whether of inventory or capacity to produce them.

4. Consider the nature of the supplier relationship

JIT production systems assume suppliers work together, but in a global supply chain, supplier relations range from being deeply collaborative to purely transactional. Buffers can help protect JIT segments from noncollaborative relationships: A more distant, noncollaborative supplier requires building a bigger buffer to overcome the uncertainty of supplies to keep the JIT segment running.

That said, building a stockpile or a plant may not always be practical or even necessary. A third-party purchasing organization like Li and Fung, with many suppliers in different countries, can also ensure regular deliveries of items.

Digital Technologies Can Make JIT Networks Even More Resilient

One of the pillars of JIT is the use of kanban, a system that conveys information between processes and automatically orders parts as they are used. The original Toyota system used cards. As an item (or a box of items) was used for production at a workstation, the card accompanying it would be returned to the preceding workstation to signal demand for another item. Digital technologies have replaced the cards and have made it possible to centralize information on the flow of all items across all workstations, allowing for controls and quicker reaction to any problems or shortages.

Digital technologies—including AI, analytics, blockchain, and internet of things (IoT)—can also be used to design and operate the kind of revamped JIT network we've described. Analytics, for example, can help members of the supply chain identify common parts across product lines and design optimal buffers. Digital twins— digital models of the supply chain—can alert downstream plants about any upstream disruptions faster so they can avail themselves of the buffers more quickly. Blockchain can be employed to help supply chain partners securely share information, and IoT technology such as sensors and RFID tags or electronic product codes can help members of the network obtain an accurate, real-time understanding of inventories. Additive manufacturing (3D printing) can provide highly flexible manufacturing capacity. (Mercedes-Benz Trucks and Daimler Buses use 3D printers to manufacture plastic spare parts for their trucks and buses on demand.)

The response to the problems plaguing global supply chains is *not* to jettison the just-in-time approach to inventory and production. It is to change the system so it can better handle uncertainties. The JIT network model we have described can help companies do that.

TAKEAWAYS

Supply chain disruptions have called into question the viability of just-in-time (JIT) global supply chains, suggesting companies shift to "just-in-case" systems that maintain lots of inventory at various locations to ensure business continuity. But instead of abandoning JIT supply chains, companies should redesign them. Here's how:

- ✓ **Map your supply chain extensively.** While all companies know who their immediate suppliers are, many don't know their lower-tier suppliers. By mapping, you can identify what parts or raw materials are most vulnerable.

- ✓ **Identify segments that can be run on a JIT basis.** Requisite conditions include minimum fluctuations in demand, matching manufacturing cycle times across the nodes in the segment, and proximity of these nodes.

- ✓ **Create buffers at the points where segments meet.** These buffers can comprise some combination of inventory, spare or backup capacity, redundant suppliers, and facilities shared with other companies.

- ✓ **Consider the nature of your supplier relationships.** A more distant, noncollaborative supplier requires building a bigger buffer to overcome the uncertainty of supplies.

Adapted from content posted on hbr.org, October 20, 2022 (product #H077UL).

SMALL BUSINESSES PLAY A BIG ROLE IN SUPPLY CHAIN RESILIENCE

by Karen G. Mills, Elisabeth B. Reynolds, and Morgane Herculano

T roy, COO of an overhead crane services company, hung up the phone and shot a worried look at the backlog of orders on his desk. An important customer had just confirmed requirements for two large industrial overhead cranes. In normal times he would be delighted, but with a 12-month backlog totaling nearly $100 million, the company was facing a dilemma. Given the disruptions and delays in his own supply chain, the strong temptation was to increase orders to be sure at least some of the parts he was waiting for might be delivered on time. But he recalled the Beer Game, a business simulation exercise developed at MIT: Students in a beer-keg supply chain simulation ordered more and more from their distributors (at higher and higher prices) until the famous bullwhip effect set in, bankrupting the student teams.[1] Troy was determined to resist the urge to over-order from his suppliers, but he knew something must change. Was there a way to create better partnerships and streamline his supply chain, creating win-win outcomes?

Troy's experience is a familiar one currently facing companies around the world. Global disruptions have wreaked havoc on supply chains over the past few years. While there are some signs of improvement, the reality is that it takes a long time for disrupted supply chains to get back on track. As David Simchi-Levi of MIT has shown in his work on semiconductor supply chains, a 10-day disruption in a firm's production leads to at least 300 days before its inventory is back to normal.[2]

The United States has an opportunity to do more than just get its supply chains back on track. It can prevent future disruptions by fundamentally improving how they operate. The key is to focus on small and midsize businesses that are critical to supply chains but that typically lag in costly technology investments—particularly enterprise software and advanced manufacturing innovations. The result is a lack of real-time operating connectivity between supply chain partners and their customers, leading to lower efficiency for the whole system. Research by MIT's Daron Acemoglu and colleagues has shown that in the United States, small and midsize enterprise productivity is a full two-thirds lower than that of larger firms, in part due to their lack of investment in new technology.[3]

The importance of small and midsize businesses in supply chains goes far beyond a few key products or industries. Supply chain companies—defined as those that sell their output primarily business-to-business (B2B)—represent about 44% of U.S. private employment. According to Karen Mills's research with Mercedes Delgado of Copenhagen Business School, these companies have an outsized impact on U.S. innovation, accounting for most of the country's STEM jobs and patents (see figure 4-1). They represent a large share of highly skilled workers, with wages 66% higher on average than those in business-to-consumer (B2C) industries. And these businesses are largely small and midsized companies, not Goliaths. Companies with fewer than 500 employees

FIGURE 4-1

The supply chain economy versus the business-to-consumer economy

The supply chain economy is a major source of innovation and high-paying jobs.

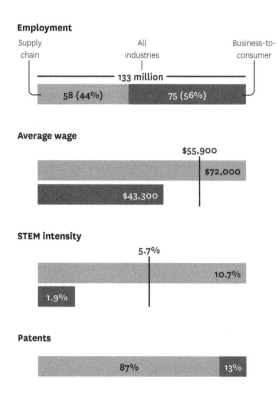

Employment

Supply chain — All industries — Business-to-consumer

133 million

58 (44%)   75 (56%)

Average wage

$55,900

$72,000

$43,300

STEM intensity

5.7%

10.7%

1.9%

Patents

87%   13%

Note: Job and wage data are from 2019; patent and STEM intensity are from 2015.

Source: Mercedes Delgado and Karen G. Mills, "The Supply Chain Economy: A New Industry Categorization for Understanding Innovation in Services," 2020.

make up 98% of supply chain firms and over 20% of U.S. private employment.

These companies represent an enormous opportunity to improve supply chain resilience while also increasing overall competitiveness. To do this, we have four recommendations.

Invest more in new technology by small and midsize suppliers

Digital transformation—the collection and sharing of real-time data within firms and with customers—will define successful supply chains in the 21st century by enabling greater inventory visibility, demand planning, and traceability. Software such as Enterprise Resource Planning systems (ERPs), Cloud Product Lifecycle Management, and "digital threads" across supply chains can smooth information flows. In addition, investments in advanced manufacturing technologies such as 3D printing, robotics, and AI-driven technologies such as predictive maintenance can help make suppliers more productive and supply chains more resilient and sustainable. Of course, these investments are not just about layering in digital technology: They require organizational restructuring as well.

Increase training to reskill and upskill workers

On today's new factory floor, digital information can be made available in real time to frontline workers so they can become knowledgeable problem-solvers, using technology to improve quality and output. But to realize that vision, companies need digitally savvy workers. Companies must invest in their workforce, but national and regional workforce training programs can also help to create a larger pipeline of digitally skilled workers—especially for smaller firms with fewer resources to invest in training.

Improve access to capital and create demand assurances

Better access to financing can help "lubricate" supply chains when there are delays and shortages as well as support investments in new technology. For example, customers can help suppliers by accelerating their payment timelines, advancing partial payments before final delivery, and by providing financing vehicles that help smaller suppliers access lower-cost capital based on supply chain relationships. In addition, customers can provide demand guarantees that give smaller suppliers more assurance before they invest in new technology. Companies cite the high costs as the main factor limiting wider adoption of new technologies. These guarantees can improve their access to credit to pay for needed technology upgrades. An example is Additive Manufacturing Forward (AM Forward), where companies make firm commitments to buy 3D-printed products from their suppliers, providing a solid demand signal that supports the supplier's investments.

Use new legislation as an opportunity to invest in smaller supply chain companies

The global economic landscape is changing due to the disruption of global supply chains, the threat of climate change, and geopolitical dynamics. Simultaneously, in the past decade we've seen major advances in digitalization that are transforming offices, factory floors, and supply chains. Partly in response to these forces, the United States has enacted three major pieces of federal legislation: the Bipartisan Infrastructure Law, the bipartisan CHIPS and Science Act, and the Inflation Reduction Act.

These investments, totaling over $1 trillion in physical infrastructure, digital and semiconductor capacity, and clean energy over the next decade, present a massive opportunity to rebuild the country's industrial base, including through more efficient, sustainable, and resilient domestic supply chains. Some of the funding provides incentives that will benefit small and midsize supply chain firms (including a doubling of the R&D payroll tax credit). Yet, the goals and ambitions of this legislation will not be achieved unless suppliers and their customers step up and make crucial technology investments and improve their connectivity, collaboration, and trust.

Troy knew that he would not solve his supply chain challenges overnight. Nonetheless he remained optimistic. The challenges of recent years highlighted that confrontational, disconnected, arm's-length supplier relationships of the past needed to change. "I told my suppliers if we exchange information real time, sync our payments schedules, and move forward with new technology, then all of us can have a win-win," Troy explained. And a win for these supply chain companies strengthens U.S. productivity, resilience, and global competitiveness.

TAKEAWAYS

Small and midsize companies are essential to U.S. supply chains, but they lag in productivity and technology adoption. Government and industry can help these smaller supply chain firms—and make supply chains significantly more resilient—by doing the following:

✓ **Invest more in new technologies.** Implementing new software across supply chains can smooth information flows, while investments in advanced manufacturing technologies can help improve productivity and sustainability.

✓ **Increase training to reskill and upskill workers.** National and regional workforce training programs can help create a larger pipeline of digitally skilled workers—especially for smaller firms with fewer training resources.

✓ **Improve access to capital and create demand assurances.** Better access to financing can help lubricate supply chains when there are delays and shortages as well as support technology investments.

✓ **Use new legislation as an opportunity to invest in smaller companies.** New federal legislation offers the chance to rebuild the U.S.'s industrial base and provide incentives that will benefit small and midsize supply chain firms.

NOTES

1. Hau L. Lee, V. Padmanabhan, and Seungjin Whang, "Information Distortion in a Supply Chain: The Bullwhip Effect," *Management Science* 43, no. 4 (April 1997): 546–558.

2. David Simchi-Levi, Feng Zhu, and Matthew Loy, "Fixing the U.S. Semiconductor Supply Chain," hbr.org, October 25, 2022, https://hbr.org/2022/10/fixing-the-u-s-semiconductor-supply -chain.

3. Daron Acemoglu et al., "Automation and the Workforce: A Firm-Level View from the 2019 Annual Business Survey" (conference paper, National Bureau of Economic Research, March 17–18, 2022), https://www.nber.org/books-and-chapters/technology -productivity-and-economic-growth/automation-and-workforce -firm-level-view-2019-annual-business-survey.

Adapted from content posted on hbr.org, December 6, 2022 (product #H07DH7).

REGIONALISM, GLOBALISM, OR BOTH?

5

LEVERAGING NEW TECH TO BRING SUPPLY CHAIN CLOSER TO HOME

by Suketu Gandhi

T he location of low-cost labor largely shaped today's
global supply chains, but that has changed dramatically over the past five years. Technology is finally
ready to replace human labor across a broad range of
supply chain activities, which will give companies more
opportunities to operate where they choose and reduce
their dependence on Asia.

Savvy companies are busily exploring how they can employ a host of new technologies to make their end-to-end supply chain much more resilient yet still competitively cost-efficient. Those that succeed will take an artificial-intelligence-plus-human intelligence (AI + HI) approach. But first, they will revisit what customers really value and bring the supply chains for higher-margin products closer to home.

The Current Challenge

Today's global supply chains were designed to operate reliably, at the lowest possible cost in a steady-state environment. Lately, however, they have been unreliable (such as with the microchip shortage) and expensive (including higher costs for labor, commodities, and ocean shipping), primarily because conditions have been anything but steady.[1] Geopolitical tensions between the Western democracies and the autocracies of Russia and China have led to calls for companies to become less vulnerable by radically restructuring their distant supply chains.

Companies have long expressed interest in reshoring, near-shoring (switching to suppliers closer to the markets served), and friend-shoring (using suppliers located in countries with shared values)—all of which offer certain logistical, strategic, and brand image advantages. The biggest obstacles have been labor costs, labor availability, and deep manufacturing expertise. The largest and most affordable pool of qualified manufacturing labor is in China and other Asian low-cost countries.

But advances in technology are starting to lower these barriers.

New Technologies

A few developments are beginning to make a difference. For example, it is possible to locate affordable factories closer to home. Companies are also improving their operations and reducing the time it takes to train workers from months to days on tasks such as assembling diverse products—electrical or mechanical—on the same assembly line.

AI + HI. The maturity of AI, particularly humans' ability to use it, offers new ways out of the cost trap. Major advances in *cobots*—robots that directly interact with humans in manufacturing facilities—combine AI and HI to lower the labor costs while retaining the value of human oversight.

3D printing. Advances in additive manufacturing (3D printing) are making it possible for companies to affordably produce a broad range of components and products. They also allow them to shorten manufacturing processes in factories closer to home, reducing reliance on numerous and distant suppliers.

Recognition technology. In manual manufacturing processes, such as automobile engine assembly, AI-driven action recognition technology combines live video with analytics to ensure that workers are correctly following complicated steps without making errors. The result is better quality control, higher productivity, and data sets that can be used to improve processes.

Digital manufacturing solutions. These systems track product manufacturing across workstations, enable real-time input of data by workers, provide end-to-end traceability, and ensure that only high-quality parts move downstream.

Three-dimensional simulations. These include metaverse applications such as NVIDIA Omniverse. Simulations allow manufacturers to build digital twins of their processes and simulate factory layouts, workstation designs, and assembly design.

Logistics technology. Investments are pouring into this area, especially in tools for warehouse management, matching freight loads to transportation capacity, and cost-effective routing. The rate of investment from venture capital (VC) firms suggests that VC funding for "supply tech" will overtake that for fintech before the end of this decade.

Three moves can help companies take full advantage of these labor-saving intelligent technologies.

Rethink what customers really value

Start with deep analysis of what customers will want, where they will want it, and when. Many products are complex in places where consumers do not see value but production is labor-intensive—issues that mattered less when supply chains were stable and labor costs low. Recognizing this, some companies are moving toward making products in smaller batches that are keyed to refined customer preferences. Some are finding ways to adapt or redesign products for automated production without sacrificing perceived or effective end-user value.

Consider an industrial tools manufacturer that had seen its products grow more complex with many subcomponents, such as motors, switches, controllers, and wiring, and many raw materials such as resins, plastics, and copper. Before bringing manufacturing from Asia and closer to most of their customers in North America and Europe, the company took a hard look at what its customers really cared about. It found that, above all, users wanted a motor that lasted a long time and a tool that could survive in a harsh operating environment. The company was able to eliminate many of its products' superfluous elements, making manufacturing easier to automate and less expensive while still delivering the attributes that customers want.

Rebalance machine intelligence with human agency

AI, analytics, and robotics can greatly reduce reliance on human effort to move products through value chains faster, more reliably, and more efficiently. But the goal should not be to remove human beings completely from processes; it should be to free them to do what they do best: make critical judgments based on their experience and expertise. For example, these technologies can allow workers to devote more time to investigating and learning from system failures and figuring out how to make the system more robust.

Consider a medical device manufacturer. In its industry, safety is the number one priority, and getting the product to the customer rapidly is number two. There is tension between these priorities. Reshoring would help get products to customers faster but increase labor costs. So the company adopted machine learning and state-of-the-art cameras to inspect for anomalies in the products and in the manufacturing process. The company's best human experts then identify the causes.

Bring newer, higher-margin products closer to home first

When companies first began moving manufacturing to low-cost countries, they usually focused first on their high-volume, lower-margin products. Now, as they relocate production closer to home and to customers, they should begin with their higher-margin products for three reasons.

First, because higher-margin products are often more complex (such as medical devices), using new technologies to produce them and to manage their supply chains can generate the most benefits.

Second, in the face of today's uncertain global supply chains, companies should consider the risks of disruptions for all of their products and make the repatriation of those that deliver the highest return the priority.

Third, thin margins leave no financial room for experimentation, learning, and the initial capital expenditure needed to maneuver in a world of new technology and higher labor costs. As a result, it's difficult to make the business case for relocation, and companies are incapable of moving forward. But when relocation is considered in terms of the total amount of margin repatriated, instead of total cost savings, the business case becomes compelling. And as a company continually improves its manufacturing proficiency with higher-margin products, it can then turn its attention to relocating the manufacture of lower-margin products.

Admittedly, making all these changes will take time. Companies will not be able to drastically reduce their dependence on suppliers in China and other distant countries overnight. But by understanding the capabilities of these technologies and aggressively investing in them, companies will be able to bolster the resilience of their supply chains in the months and years ahead.

TAKEAWAYS

The location of low-cost labor largely shaped today's global supply chains, but that has changed dramatically. Technology is ready to replace human labor across a broad range of supply chain activities, which will give companies more opportunities to operate where they choose.

✓ New advancements in technology—including AI + HI, 3D printing, recognition technology, digital manufacturing solutions, and 3D simulations—are making it possible for Western countries to relocate factories closer to home, lowering supply chain risk.

✓ To remove complexity from supply chains, companies should rethink what customers really value and simplify products' superfluous elements.

✓ Companies should bring higher-margin products closer to home first. Higher-margin products are typically more complex and more exposed to supply chain risk.

NOTE

1. Jason Furman and Wilson Powell III, "Record U.S. Productivity Slump in First Half of 2022 Risks Higher Inflation and Unemployment," *PIIE* (blog), August 9, 2022, https://www.piie.com/blogs/realtime-economics/record-us-productivity-slump-first-half-2022-risks-higher-inflation-and; CMO Pink Sheet, September 2022, World Bank, https://thedocs.worldbank.org/en/doc/5d903e848d b1d1b83e0ec8f744e55570-0350012021/related/CMO-Pink-Sheet

-September-2022.pdf; Yan Carrière-Swallow et al., "How Soaring Shipping Cost Raise Prices Around the World," *IMF* (blog), March 28, 2022, https://www.imf.org/en/Blogs/Articles/2022/03/28/how-soaring-shipping-costs-raise-prices-around-the-world.

Adapted from "Leveraging New Tech to Boost Supply Chain Resilience," on hbr.org, October 26, 2022 (product #H079ZF).

6

TRADE REGIONALIZATION: MORE HYPE THAN REALITY?

by Steven A. Altman and Caroline R. Bastian

For more than a decade, experts have been predicting a shift to more-regionalized trade patterns, as companies adopt near-shoring strategies to produce goods closer to the markets where they will be sold. Many expected Covid-19 to turbocharge this trend.

But recent data suggests a more skeptical take on trade regionalization. Trade flows have stretched out over *longer* distances, even during the pandemic.[1] While trade regionalization may increase moving forward, we wouldn't bet on a transformational shift from global to regional business.

The Elusive Evidence of Rising Regionalization

In our DHL Global Connectedness Index 2021 Update report, we track the percentage of world merchandise trade taking place within regions using four different regional definitions: one each from the World Trade Organization (WTO) and United Nations, as well as by continent and within the three macroregions of Asia-Pacific, EMEA (Europe, Middle East, and Africa), and the Americas.

While there was a clear trend toward *less* regionalized trade between 2003 and 2012, no consistent trend appears in more recent years. When we use the WTO's definition, which divides the world into seven regions, we do find an increase in regional trade between 2012 and 2016.[2] But that trend *ended* in 2016. And if we divide the world up using the other three regional definitions, the rising trend disappears entirely. (See figure 6-1.)

Since all region definitions involve subjective judgments, we prefer to focus on a more objective measure of

FIGURE 6-1

Limited evidence of increased trade regionalization

To examine whether trade became more regional, the authors calculated the share of trade within regions using different region definitions. While there was a trend toward less regionalized trade between 2003 and 2012, no consistent trend appears in more recent years.

Merchandise trade
Percent intraregional, by region classifications

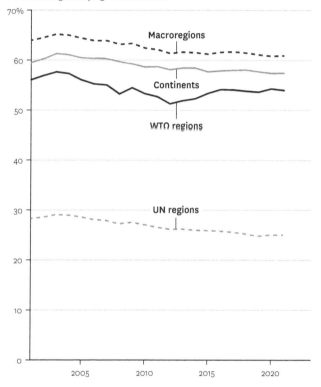

Three macroregions: Americas; Asia; Europe, Middle East, and Africa (EMEA)

Six continents: Africa; Asia; Europe; North America; Oceania; South America

Seven WTO regions: Africa; Asia; Commonwealth of Independent States (CIS); Europe; Middle East; North America; South and Central America and the Caribbean

Twenty-two UN regions: Australia and New Zealand; Caribbean; Central America; Central Asia; Eastern Africa; Eastern Asia; Eastern Europe; Melanesia; Micronesia; Middle Africa; Northern Africa; Northern America; Northern Europe; Polynesia; South America; South-Eastern Asia; Southern Africa; Southern Asia; Southern Europe; Western Africa; Western Asia; Western Europe

Source: IMF Direction of Trade Statistics (DOTS).

shifts in global trade patterns: the average distance traversed by all trade flows around the world.

If there really was a robust shift toward regionalization, one would expect trade, on average, to take place over *shorter* distances. But our analysis for the 2022 DHL Global Connectedness Index found that trade flows have actually stretched out over *longer* distances since 2004, albeit with a pause between 2012 and 2018 (see figure 6-2).

The Pandemic Increased Long-Distance Trade

Trade has even traversed longer distances during the Covid-19 pandemic, despite expectations that disruptions would force greater reliance on nearby suppliers.[3] This is because exports grew strongly in Asia to meet growing demand for imported goods in many parts of the world.[4] Therefore, countries far away from Asia imported over longer distances, while countries within Asia itself imported over shorter distances (see figure 6-3). This overall shift to more long-distance trade advanced even as some buyers did switch to closer suppliers, especially for time-sensitive products. While disruptions to long-distance trade dominated the headlines, short-distance trade was also hampered by pandemic-induced capacity bottlenecks and labor shortages.

FIGURE 6-2

Trade flows are stretching over longer distances

Between 2004 and 2021, the average distance traversed by merchandise trade has increased from about 4,550 km (2,830 miles) to almost 5,100 km (3,170 miles).

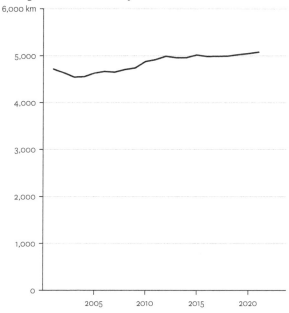

Average distance traversed by merchandise trade

Sources: IMF Direction of Trade Statistics (DOTS), CEPII GeoDist.

FIGURE 6-3

Change in average distance traversed by merchandise imports by region

In 2020, exports grew strongly in Asia to meet the growing demand for imported goods in many parts of the world. Therefore, countries far away from Asia imported over longer distances, while countries within Asia itself imported over shorter distances.

Merchandise imports
By region, in US$ trillions

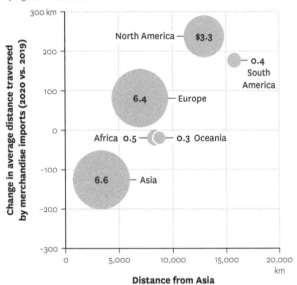

Note: Circles are proportional to the value of each region's imports in 2019. Distance from Asia is measured based on the population-weighted distance between major cities in each region. Asia's own distance from Asia is greater than zero because of the distance between Asian cities.

Sources: UN Comtrade, IMF Direction of Trade Statistics (DOTS), CEPII GeoDist.

The fact that long-distance trade grew more during the pandemic than short-distance trade raises questions about the role of regionalization in strategies for reducing supply chain risk. Near-shoring and regionalization have many attractions, and they can increase resilience via shorter transit times and reduced cross-region interdependencies.

But long-distance trade can also contribute to resilience. Long-distance trade boosts specialization and scale economies, and there is some evidence that producers were able to ramp up exports faster during the pandemic in countries that supply a large share of global demand for their products.[5]

Regionalization in the Long Run?

Looking forward, geopolitical tensions, technological trends, and environmental concerns all have the potential to contribute to an increase in trade regionalization. So could new trade blocs such as the Regional Comprehensive Economic Partnership (in the Asia-Pacific region) and the African Continental Free Trade Area. And pandemic-induced supply chain regionalization might gather pace in the coming years, because major reconfigurations take time to execute.

Nonetheless, other forces will continue to favor long-distance trade. These include container shipping costs eventually coming down to more normal levels, the growing share of emerging economies in global trade (they tend to trade over longer distances), and the ongoing improvement of technologies that ease long-distance transactions.

Waning business interest in regionalization, after a spike at the beginning of the pandemic, also reinforces the sense that predictions of a major increase in regional trade could fail to materialize. In an April 2020 survey, 83% of executives said their companies planned on near-shoring to regionalize their supply chains. When the same survey was repeated in March–April 2021, only 23% still said they were planning on near-shoring.[6] Another set of surveys shows that companies have backed off from regionalization and near-shoring plans and instead have embraced other ways of increasing supply chain resilience, such as increasing inventory levels and dual-sourcing raw materials.[7]

The war in Ukraine has given another boost to business interest in regionalization. However, many of the war's effects, so far, have favored long-distance trade. The European Union, for example, is increasing energy imports from more distant countries to reduce its dependence on Russia. Meanwhile, Russia is trading more with Asia instead of Europe, despite the greater distance from Russia's major population centers.[8]

The potential for large increases in trade regionalization is also constrained by the fact that trade is already quite regionalized. Using most regional definitions, more than half of world trade happens inside regions, roughly three times the proportion one would expect in a "frictionless" world where distance and cross-country differences did not affect trade patterns.[9] Surprisingly, transportation costs explain less than 30% of the dampening effect of distance on trade.[10] Preferences for similar products in neighboring countries, regional trade agreements, and many other similarities and linkages among proximate countries have long boosted short-distance trade.

Should Your Company Embrace Regionalization?

The main implication of this analysis is that leaders should be skeptical about the assumption that a major regionalization wave is under way. If your company is contemplating regionalization because you expect your customers or suppliers to embrace regional strategies, take a careful look at what actual commitments they are making, since the rhetoric about regionalization may have gotten ahead of the reality.

Ultimately, the main drivers of whether or not a company should regionalize should be the economic fundamentals that have always guided such decisions, most importantly demand patterns and production costs/capabilities.

What *is* new is the extent to which companies should factor geopolitical tensions into their thinking. The near-shoring trend may fall short of expectations, but what many are starting to call friend-shoring or ally-shoring could become increasingly important in strategically sensitive industries.

Be especially careful of any supply chain reconfigurations that could lock in a higher cost structure for your company. Without sustained government support, a company that significantly increases its cost base risks losing business to more efficient competitors. And while the pandemic and the war in Ukraine have put a spotlight on the need for resilience, they have also contributed to a large rise in inflation and strained government budgets. This implies that substantial policy support for relocating supply chains will be limited to the most politically sensitive product categories. Rising pressure to reduce costs will require companies to look near *and* far for the most efficient and reliable production and sourcing locations.

TAKEAWAYS

Experts have been predicting a shift from global trade toward more regionalized patterns. However, a recent analysis of trade data shows a clear trend toward less regionalized trade between 2003 and 2012, and no consistent trend in more recent years.

✓ Since 2004, trade flows have generally stretched over longer distances. This trend increased during the pandemic.

✓ While geopolitical tensions, technological trends, and environmental concerns all have the potential to contribute to an increase in trade regionalization, other forces, such as decreased container shipping costs and the ongoing improvement of technologies that ease long-distance transactions, will continue to favor long-distance trade.

✓ When deciding whether to regionalize, leaders should focus on the economic fundamentals that have always guided such decisions—most importantly, demand patterns and production costs/capabilities.

✓ Companies *should* factor geopolitical tensions into their thinking; friend-shoring or ally-shoring could become increasingly important in strategically sensitive industries.

NOTES

1. Steven A. Altman and Caroline R. Bastian, "DHL Global Connectedness Index 2021 Update," Deutsche Post DHL Group, November 2021, https://www.dhl.com/content/dam/dhl/global/dhl-spotlight/documents/pdf/2021-gci-update-report.pdf.

2. "Compositions, Definitions, and Methodology," *World Trade Statistical Review 2018*, World Trade Organization, http://webservices.wto.org/resources/meta/def_method_e.pdf.

3. OECD, "International Trade During the Covid-19 Pandemic: Big Shifts and Uncertainty," OECD, March 10, 2022, https://www.oecd.org/coronavirus/policy-responses/international-trade-during-the-covid-19-pandemic-big-shifts-and-uncertainty-d1131663/.

4. Christine Arriola, Przemyslaw Kowalski, and Frank van Tongeren, "The Impact of Covid-19 on Directions and Structure of International Trade," OECD Trade Policy Papers, September 20, 2021, https://www.oecd-ilibrary.org/trade/the-impact-of-covid-19-on-directions-and-structure-of-international-trade_0b8eaafe-en; Harriet Torry, "Consumer Demand for Goods Drove U.S. Import Surge During Holidays," *Wall Street Journal*, January 6, 2022, https://www.wsj.com/articles/consumer-demand-for-goods-likely-drove-u-s-import-surge-during-holidays-11641465001.

5. Arriola et al., "The Impact of Covid-19 on Directions and Structure of International Trade."

6. Julie Linn Teigland, Marc Lhermitte, and Hanne Jesca Bax, "How Can Europe Reset the Investment Agenda Now to Rebuild Its Future?" EY, May 28, 2020, https://www.ey.com/en_gl/attractiveness/20/how-can-europe-reset-the-investment-agenda-now-to-rebuild-its-future; Julie Linn Teigland, Hanne Jesca Bax, and Marc Lhermitte, "Foreign Investors Back Europe, but Is Europe Back?" EY, June 7, 2021, https://www.ey.com/en_us/attractiveness/21/foreign-investors-back-europe-but-is-europe-back.

7. Knut Alicke, Ed Barriball, and Vera Trautwein, "How Covid-19 Is Reshaping Supply Chains," McKinsey & Company, November 23, 2021, https://www.mckinsey.com/capabilities/operations/our-insights/how-covid-19-is-reshaping-supply-chains.

8. Brendan Murray and Bryce Baschuk, "Europe Seeks to Redraw Trade Routes as War Strains Alliances," Bloomberg, May 5, 2022, https://www.bloomberg.com/news/newsletters/2022-05-05/supply-chain-latest-europe-seeks-to-speed-free-trade-deals.

9. Steven A. Altman and Caroline R. Bastian, "Connecting to the World," DHL, n.d., https://www.dhl.com/content/dam/dhl/global/dhl-spotlight/documents/pdf/10-years-lessons-gci-2021-report.pdf.

10. Keith Head and Thierry Mayer, "What Separates Us? Sources of Resistance to Globalization," *Canadian Journal of Economics* 46, no. 4 (2013): 1196–1231.

Adapted from content posted on hbr.org, May 31, 2022 (product #H071ZC).

Section 3

INNOVATION IN YOUR SUPPLY CHAIN

7

A BETTER WAY TO MATCH SUPPLY AND DEMAND IN THE RETAIL SUPPLY CHAIN

by Mike Doherty and George Stalk Jr.

T he ongoing supply chain crisis threatens the success of retailers and their suppliers because its volatility makes both overstocks (having something customers don't want) and stockouts (running out of the items they desire) more likely. And the stakes are high: Stockouts can cost retailers their total gross margin. Overstocks, if they are lucky, cost retailers 50% of their gross margins but more likely, all the margins.

A methodology we call *flow-casting* offers a way to escape the drag on profits of overstocks and stockouts. Flow-casting is different from forecasting. It develops only a forecast of sales to end users at the retail store level (that is, consumers), and this forecast is then used to calculate all demand and inventory flows for each element upstream in the supply chain. It is designed to plan inventory, replenishment, space, and resource requirements throughout the retail supply chain over a long-term planning horizon (typically 52 weeks or more). The key is these projections are updated daily or weekly and provided to all elements of the supply chain simultaneously.

Having all players in the supply chain use demand projections based on a forecast of end-customer demand differs from the way most supply chains in the retail sector operate today. Currently, the elements of most supply chains see demand as orders from its direct customer, not the end consumer. As a result, each element finds itself chasing demand that does not reflect true consumer demand. This pursuit results in wild swings in perceived supply and demand along the supply chain known as the *bullwhip effect*, which drives overstocks and stockouts.

How Flow-Casting Works

The steps in developing flow-casting plans are the following:

1. The retailer generates a forecast of consumer sales, in units, that extends a year or more into the future for every item in every store, including any planned sales uplifts from promotions or other marketing initiatives.

2. The retailer's sales forecast is deducted from its current store inventory and used to calculate projected inventory levels and future shipments needed from suppliers, which the retailer shares with suppliers.

3. Based on the projections, all elements of the supply chain calculate required labor, space, equipment, and capital resources necessary to acquire, make, transport, store, and deliver products from the final point of manufacture to the final point of sale.

This process can be done manually but it's best if it's automated—first at the retailer and then throughout the supply chain. That said, some smaller suppliers may simply input the projections into the spreadsheets they use for planning.

This system provides retailers and their suppliers with a new kind of visibility—a forward-looking, daily, or weekly projection of demand, supply, and inventory by item and location. The implications for retailers and their suppliers are significant. Flow-casting not only eliminates the need for suppliers to forecast their retail trading partners' needs, but also ensures that the unified supply-and-demand picture along the entire supply chain is being resynchronized daily. By doing so, it greatly reduces overstocks and stockouts and substantially minimizes the bullwhip effect.

If there is some aspect of the future that might impact sales or inventory, it's in the flow-casting plans. For example, suppose a retailer plans to open several new stores. These stores would have a sales forecast by product, which would be included in the flow-casting plans.

Flow-casting is best initiated by the retailer. However, if you are a key supplier to a retailer, you can take the initiative to jump-start the flow-casting methodology. For example, a key supplier to one of the largest discount retailers used information from the retailer's point-of-sales data (with the retailer's cooperation) to develop a flowcast for the retailer by store to the retailer's distribution center to the supplier's distribution center to the supplier's factory. This retailer experienced improvements in in-stocks (to 99% from 97%) and a 20% reduction in overstocks.

The Risks and the Costs

The risk in transitioning to flow-casting is that companies fail to understand that this is a process and mindset change, and therefore the transition needs to be managed as a change-management initiative, not just a technology upgrade. That requires people within the retailer and supplier network be educated, trained, coached, and supported as they learn and gradually grow accustomed to the new ways of working.

This transition usually takes two to three years—primarily because large retailers have hundreds of key suppliers and thousands overall. Flow-casting should be run in a simulation mode prior to becoming operational so that all essential stakeholders in the retailer and at key suppliers can see what the system's projections based only on forecasts of consumer sales look like, giving everyone time to minimize surprises when the system goes live.

The investments to implement flow-casting include the costs of new technology, system integration, data integrity efforts (like cleansing sales history for abnormal selling periods and events such as weather-related interruptions), teaching people the concepts of the approach, training them how to use technology to execute the process, and supporting them. In our experience this has amounted to less than a quarter of 1% of annual sales.

Flow-Casting in Action

Princess Auto, a retailer of automotive aftermarket parts and related products and tools that has over 50 stores throughout Canada, is an early adopter of flow-casting. Its stores consistently achieve daily *in-stocks* (that is, customers can find the items they want to buy) of 97% to 98%, up from 92% in 2015—even during promotional periods and, importantly, for products from both domestic and offshore suppliers.

In 2016, the first year that the company used the flow-casting system, its sales increased by more than 10% because of improved in-stocks. (We have generally found that every 2% to 3% increase in in-stock performance results in a sales increase of at least 1%.) Both Princess Auto's store and distribution centers' inventories decreased by more than 10%.

Retailers interested in obtaining the benefits of flow-casting should start by assessing the impact, benefits, and challenges of using this approach. Since flow-casting improves in-stocks and reduces overstocks, the added profits it generates significantly outstrip its costs, and it leads to more satisfied consumers.

TAKEAWAYS

In the face of supply chain volatility, traditional methods of forecasting are falling short for retailers and their suppliers. Instead, retailers should depend on another approach: flow-casting.

✓ In flow-casting, the retailer generates a forecast of consumer sales, in units, that extends a year or more into the future for every item in every store.

✓ The retailer's sales forecast is deducted from its current store inventory and used to calculate projected inventory levels and future shipments needed from suppliers, which the retailer shares with suppliers.

✓ All elements of the supply chain calculate required labor, space, equipment, and capital resources necessary to acquire, make, transport, store, and deliver products from the final point of manufacture to the final point of sale.

✓ This process can be done manually but it is best automated—first at the retailer, then throughout the supply chain.

Adapted from content posted on hbr.org, December 1, 2022 (product #H07DO1).

8

HOW TO TURN A SUPPLY CHAIN PLATFORM INTO AN INNOVATION ENGINE

by Kasra Ferdows, Hau L. Lee, and Xiande Zhao

I n early February 2020, when its home country of China was coping with the first wave of Covid-19, Haier Group, one of the world's largest manufacturers of home appliances, faced a challenge and an opportunity. A customer—Heji Home, a Chinese home-furnishings company—asked Haier for help in producing mobile isolation wards that it wished to donate to a hospital in

Wuhan, the site of the first outbreak of the novel coronavirus. These units required fresh-air, sterilization, and sewage-treatment systems that met stringent medical standards. Neither company had produced such equipment before, and neither had the design resources and supply chain capabilities necessary to go it alone. So they teamed up, and despite widespread lockdowns because of the pandemic and other business closings for the Chinese New Year, they managed to develop a working prototype of the unit and deliver it to the hospital in two weeks. That was quickly followed by the production and delivery of additional units to local hospitals in the subsequent weeks. Heji and Haier continued their collaboration and in the ensuing months developed other versions of the unit, such as a mobile nucleic-acid testing station and a mobile vaccination station, to meet new demands.

Such agility required that the two companies quickly identify the right partners in several industries, including industrial appliances, health care, and construction, and that all the parties involved trust one another and be willing to collaborate on the design. Haier and Heji Home were able to get a prototype built and tested, configure the supply chain, and line up manufacturing capacity in a matter of weeks—all because of Haier's digital platform.

COSMOPlat (which stands for Cloud of Smart Manu-facturing Operation Platform) is fundamentally different from conventional digital supply chain platforms and other types of digital platforms. It facilitates a broader range of collaborations—from innovation and design to supplying materials and components to solving techni-cal problems and providing new services—and can be used by any of its members to mobilize responses to new opportunities or cope with disruptions. What's more, platform membership is not limited to Haier's suppliers. It includes companies that its suppliers have invited to join and others whose employees have heard about the platform from colleagues at conferences and professional meetings and from stories in the media. Haier is plan-ning to make COSMOPlat a stand-alone business that offers services to companies in other industries.

Many companies would benefit from having a digital platform with capabilities like Haier's. In this article, we offer an overview of how Haier developed COSMOPlat, examine how it differs from digital platforms used by other multinationals, describe how Haier and its suppli-ers leverage the information and relationships created by the platform to solve problems quickly, and provide guidance to companies that aspire to create a similar platform.

How Haier's Platform Is Different

Haier's digital platform was created in 2012 to improve the company's basic procurement functions. The early versions were designed to place orders, coordinate production plans, and manage inventories, payments, and other routine transactions. However, Zhang Ruimin, Haier's founder and CEO, soon decided that he wanted the platform to go beyond facilitating routine supply chain functions and be able to mobilize critical resources inside and outside the company. He hoped to increase the agility of the supply chain—by helping to solve problems such as supply disruptions, unexpected shifts in demand, and quality issues—and to seize new opportunities quickly and efficiently. Accordingly, the company began adding new capabilities to the platform and changed its name to COSMOPlat in 2016.

Haier has deployed COSMOPlat in some 20 countries, and although its direct benefits are difficult to quantify, senior management believes that it has been instrumental in achieving substantial gains in the form of shorter order-to-delivery times, greater production efficiency, reduced stockout rates, faster receipt of payments, and increased capability for product customization. Other member companies report that COSMOPlat has helped them significantly. Compaks RV, a manufacturer of motor homes, camping trailers, and recreational vehicles based in Rongcheng, China, reduced its production cycle from 35 to 20 days, trimmed procurement costs by 7.3%, and increased customer orders by 62%. Other members, including Heji Home and Tongyi Ceramics Science and Technology, a Chinese producer of ceramic products, say that the platform has allowed them to improve performance in areas such as product development, procurement costs, production cycle times, sales, and net profits.

Over the past five years, we examined more than a dozen platforms developed by other companies and found that Haier's differs from them in significant ways. One is that COSMOPlat provides a much wider range of integrated functions to facilitate the collaboration of multiple companies up and down the value chain. Many major companies have digital platforms dedicated to supply chain management. Some advanced platforms, such as GE's Predix and Siemens's MindSphere, help members use advanced technologies, such as Industry 4.0 digital capabilities (internet of things connectivity, cloud computing, analytics, and artificial intelligence), to improve the operational efficiency of factories and products in the field. And others, such as the Taiwan Semiconductor Manufacturing Corporation's Open Innovation Platform, focus on product development—designing new chips in the case of TSMC. COSMOPlat is both a supplier management system and an innovation engine.

Developing Haier's Smart Refrigerator

Haier used COSMOPlat to orchestrate the development, production, and distribution of its smart refrigerator. Here's how.

User Input

The platform helped Haier identify design choices in just a few weeks and then get feedback from an online community of existing and potential consumers—on the preferred size of storage compartments, whether they wanted to monitor their refrigerators' contents on their phones, and so on. This revealed customer needs that Haier had not fully considered. It learned, for instance, that people keep a variety of items in the refrigerator—such as skin care products, herbal extracts, and breast milk—that require different temperatures, humidity levels, and airflows. Those insights were turned into descriptive statistics to support the design team.

Technical Expertise

The platform allowed Haier to attract qualified suppliers with the necessary capabilities in multiple tiers. For example, Haier posted on the platform that it was looking for ways to reduce air leakage between the refrigerator glass door and the door frame. Sika, a global leader in industrial adhesives, sealants, and surface treatments that had joined the platform for a different project, offered to help. Together Haier and Sika analyzed the forces acting on the door and the required bonding strength of the adhesive to arrive at a solution. Sika also helped Haier automate the application of the adhesive using a specially designed robot. The process, which normally would have taken six months, was accomplished in two.

Logistics and Service Operations

COSMOPlat gave access to many third-party providers of last-mile logistics, warehousing, and appliance maintenance and repair services. It also collected data about repairs and customers' reactions to the refrigerator. This data was available to all platform members involved in the refrigerator, which allowed them to quickly address problems—such as locating spare parts and arranging their prompt delivery to repair service personnel.

(continued)

Developing Haier's Smart Refrigerator

Product-Life-Cycle Management

Haier used COSMOPlat's "digital twin" capabilities to create virtual models of the refrigerator. In the design phase, simulations of how the product specifications and process technologies interacted helped the project team optimize both. In the production phase, the digital twin was used to monitor physical manufacturing environments to detect out-of-control processes and continuously improve machine settings. The digital twin monitors the performance of the refrigerator in people's homes and sends customers alerts to change settings to improve energy usage, reduce food wastage, and properly maintain their products. That information is available to Haier's designers for use in improving performance and optimizing settings automatically.

Another difference between Haier's platform and those of others is the extent to which it controls the supplier network. Many companies decide which suppliers may join their platform and designate the tasks they will be involved with. Haier, by contrast, does not limit membership to its own suppliers; nor does it specify who will work on what. Rather, it posts a description of a problem it is facing on COSMOPlat and lets any supplier—current or potential, even one from a different industry—offer solutions or engage in collaborative efforts to find one. Many large companies also tightly control the collaborative process, whereas Haier does not. The relevant parties work together on finding a solution without Haier's continual involvement. Such an organic approach to tapping the capabilities of other organizations and marshaling needed resources is particularly helpful when the opportunity for offering a new product or service has a short time window and the company does not already have the requisite design capabilities or suppliers, or when it faces a major or sudden disruption.

Expand the Role of Supply Chains and Platforms

Building a platform that, like COSMOPlat, is both a supply chain management system and an innovation engine requires a company's leaders to broaden their perspective. They should think of the platform as a tool for the following.

1. Enlarging the supplier network quickly

Many companies focus on improving the efficiency and agility of their current supply chains. A common approach is for an original equipment manufacturer to map out its multitier supply networks, develop information links with the network members, and create a tracking system to monitor and coordinate the flow of products and information among suppliers. But as climate- and pandemic-related disruptions have driven home in the past five years, a company may need to significantly change its existing supply chain or form a new one when a crisis occurs or a new opportunity arises. A digital platform like COSMO-Plat can greatly expedite the process of bringing in new partners—sometimes from unexpected places.

2. Looking beyond procurement

A primary goal of digitizing a supply chain is usually to manage the flow of materials and goods (such as orders, deliveries, inventories, and forecasts) and the services directly related to them (such as payments and logistics) among members of the supply network. But when opportunities arise that require the development of radically new products and services, a company may need an array of new players: those that have design and product testing capabilities, possess relevant IP, and can help rapidly ramp up production, deliver products, and provide after-sales services. A digital platform can help locate such players quickly and make it easy for them to work with one another. It is also useful in identifying and bringing on board expertise that will be helpful in developing and producing products and services just appearing on the horizon. A digital platform can help build out an expansion of the necessary capabilities—for example, 3D sampling to assess variations of new designs digitally, virtual reality to see or experience how a new design works under a range of conditions, and virtual prototyping tools to validate the physical and engineering properties and compatibilities of a new design.

3. Generating new opportunities and solutions

Ideas for new opportunities or solutions to problems can come from all parts of the ecosystem. But just providing a digital platform isn't enough to persuade members to offer solutions or participate in efforts to achieve them. They must feel confident that the collaboration will benefit them, which entails specifying the rules of engagement and the ways costs and benefits will be shared.

A Closer Look

Let's now examine the architecture of the COSMOPlat system. The platform consists of three modules.

Cooperative innovation and design

This module helps different companies collaborate in the design of products and components to ensure that they can be manufactured efficiently and transported and delivered safely and economically. It also facilitates communication and knowledge sharing. For example, a component for a new model of a home appliance may require a ceramics company and a supplier of an electronic control box to work together. This module provides protocols for the exchange of information between the design teams as they come up with solutions to technical problems. It provides templates for project management, monitors target dates for important milestones, and manages intellectual property permissions. It helps move from a prototype to large-scale production by identifying the factories with the right capacity and location, automation, quality control, and product test standards. The module can also be used to survey potential end users to get feedback on design, hear about any problems, and learn about other features that the product should include. These actions may be initiated by any COSMOPlat member—not just Haier's suppliers.

Production resources integration

This module facilitates procurement, manages orders, and coordinates the flow of materials in the production of the final product. It configures the supply chain and allows suppliers in different tiers to explore capabilities and coordinate their production capacities. It creates a detailed layout of the manufacturing process, materials handling system, and labor requirements. It also enables product feasibility testing, prototyping, and ramp-up planning. Most other supply chain management platforms lack the ability to incorporate many supply tiers and dynamically change the supply network.

Distribution and service

This module enables platform members to coordinate or integrate their individual capabilities in distribution, logistics, and after-sales services to support the needs of new products. For example, it allows them to work together to decide what marketing channels to use and how to develop the channel partners; to determine where inventories of a new product will be held (the final assembly factory, specific distribution centers, or retailers' warehouses); and to devise processes for order fulfillment and delivery. It also enables service support and repair (whether tasks should be done in-house or outsourced, how and where to store spare parts, and so on) and the management of returns.

Any company may apply to join any of these interactive modules without being formally invited by Haier or anyone else. All it needs to do is complete a questionnaire and provide documented evidence of its qualifications and capabilities. Once a company registers, Haier conducts a cursory review, which often takes only a day. That gives the company access to nonconfidential information on COSMOPlat, such as general descriptions of issues needing solutions and which members may be working on them. Instead of putting a company through a formal certification process at the outset—as many major companies do, and which can take weeks—Haier allows interested companies to explore the platform relatively painlessly. If a company wants to join a project, Haier performs a rigorous evaluation to check its production or technical capabilities and its track record on quality, pricing, and sustainability. This due diligence, which may include on-site visits, usually takes no more than a few days. If the review turns up serious problems, Haier drops the supplier and blocks it from the platform.

Haier intends to keep expanding COSMOPlat's capabilities. New functions will include energy and carbon-reduction management, digital financing, and cross-border trade services. It will also expand "digital twin" capabilities—the use of virtual models of physical objects or systems to improve how they are designed, manufactured, operated, and serviced.

Developing a Similar Platform

Creating a platform like COSMOPlat requires a company to be widely known and reputable, have experience managing multiple tiers of suppliers, and have a reasonable level of expertise in digital technologies—prerequisites that put such an initiative beyond the reach of many small and medium-size companies. The good news is that it can start small and grow gradually, without a heavy commitment of resources at the outset. As Haier did, a company can build modules that have limited functionality, gradually add more features, and then link the modules for better communications between them. It can learn by doing and use early wins—even small ones—to build confidence among both internal and external stakeholders and generate savings that can be used to help finance subsequent steps.

A digital platform like COSMOPlat can provide benefits in normal times and during crises. By enabling its members to organize and conduct work faster and more efficiently, it can alleviate the requirement for costly alternatives such as carrying large emergency stockpiles of materials, components, and final products or building extensive buffer production and logistics capacities. Equally important, it can help a company's value chain evolve organically so that it can better serve today's needs as well as those that emerge tomorrow.

TAKEAWAYS

Most companies have digital platforms that support specific functions, such as supply chain management, product design, or operations, and they tightly regulate who may join the platform. The Chinese appliance manufacturer Haier has taken a unique, open approach with its supply chain management platform, COSMOPlat.

✓ Through COSMOPlat, Haier facilitates a broad range of collaborations from innovation and design to supplying materials and components to solving technical problems and providing new services.

✓ The platform allows Haier to capitalize on the expertise and resources of its ecosystem, rapidly exploit new business opportunities, respond quickly to disruptions, and achieve efficiencies.

✓ Any company may apply to join any of COSMOPlat's interactive modules; all it needs to do is complete a questionnaire and provide documented evidence of its qualifications and capabilities.

✓ Haier intends to keep expanding COSMOPlat's capabilities, including energy and carbon-reduction management, digital financing, and cross-border trade services.

Adapted from Harvard Business Review, *July–August 2022 (product #R2204K).*

Section 4

NAVIGATING SUPPLIER RELATIONSHIPS

9

IN UNCERTAIN TIMES, BIG COMPANIES NEED TO TAKE CARE OF THEIR SUPPLIERS

by Willy C. Shih

The resilience of a supply chain depends on the reliable performance of the suppliers that comprise it, but the fiscal health of many lower-tier firms is often not visible to executives at companies several tiers up. This is especially true for original equipment manufacturers (OEMs) like automakers or industrial equipment producers that often have many lower-tier suppliers.

The problem is that many of these OEMs designed their procurement strategies and supply agreements during a time when the global geopolitical and trading environments were comparatively benign, with steady growth of cross-border trade, low inflation, and stable raw materials and logistics costs. The pandemic and the war in Ukraine have revealed many vulnerabilities of global supply chains, but the disproportionate impact on many smaller suppliers is just beginning to be revealed. It's time to revisit some of the assumptions underlying supply chain practices and redesign some of them for a new era of volatility and unpredictability.

Let's start with the principles that are the foundations of outsourcing and the practices that many OEMs have developed over the years. The motivation for outsourcing the manufacture of part or all of a product is to focus on some value-added work in-house while harnessing an outside division of labor for the rest. Outsourced suppliers often are specialists that have unique skills or capabilities that the OEM lacks. Outsourcing can lead to a better utilization of assets and reduce the capital intensity of an OEM's operations. Suppliers who do this work can, in principle, pool demand across multiple customers and achieve better scale economies. They can then share some of the cost savings in the form of lower prices passed on to their customers.

While manufacturers have outsourced parts of their production for many decades, the rapid growth in offshoring to China in the 2000s has contributed mightily to an environment of muted inflation, in spite of occasional sharp swings in commodity and energy prices. This fostered the growth of some contracting processes such as long-term fixed-price contracts with annual price reductions.

The auto industry placed additional burdens on suppliers: Contracts for vehicle components not only included quantities needed for production but also required the provision of spare parts after a model was no longer available for sale, a time that might stretch out as much as a decade or longer. If producing the part—say, a windshield—required special tooling such as molds or dies, those tools then had to be kept around as well.

Manufacturers also pushed production offshore in pursuit of lower costs. Managers at one U.S. domestic firm explained to me how a 15% savings after the higher transportation costs were factored in was sufficient to justify moving production to a Chinese supplier, and people at another U.S. manufacturer recounted how a 25% savings was sufficient to push the bulk of high-volume production there. This meant that the company lost the bulk of the production volume, and it had to sell what was left at a "pressured" (that is, lower) price.

At the same time, manufacturers pursued lean inventories and just-in-time (JIT) production, putting the burden on suppliers to hold stock by imposing punitive terms if one of their production lines had to stop because of missed deliveries. The idea was to offload risk to suppliers—the risks of material cost increases, the risks and costs associated with carrying inventory, and the risks of supply chain disruptions further upstream.

Over the last few years, even the largest firms have not been able to foresee strings of disruptive events—from semiconductor shortages and raw material shortages and cost increases to operational and logistics hurdles. Yet while U.S. automakers announced strong or record profits, many small suppliers have really struggled.

The CEO at one lower-tier supplier who didn't want to be identified told me that the price of petrochemical-based resins that it used to make plastic parts has doubled in the last year, and those resins made up 40% to 50% of the company's product costs. With its single-digit margins, it had no ability to absorb the increases, but it was unable to pass along cost increases. "They [the customer] refuse to even meet with us, and just say they have a fixed-price contract," he explained.

Another small supplier's CEO told me that while his company was tied to a 10-year fixed-cost contract, his customer, a U.S. automaker, could change suppliers at will. In the early days of the pandemic, some OEMs cut their orders on a single day's notice, leaving the company holding inventory and having to spread its employment and fixed costs over what volumes remained. This firm—

whose managers, fearing reprisals by its OEM customers, requested that it not be identified—described the Detroit OEM "standard playbook" as a string of constant threats to move their work elsewhere.

Stellantis even announced that for new purchase contracts, "all future events are deemed foreseeable" by suppliers.[1] One has to wonder if anyone could foresee the events of the past several years.

The consequences of past buying practices for supply chain resilience are clear. By driving production offshore, companies have ended up with far-flung supply lines subject to logistics disruptions and huge cost escalations. Transactional behavior toward domestic suppliers has weakened them, and in industries such as autos and aerospace, it has driven consolidation. This ultimately weakens OEMs' bargaining power, while reducing the diversity of their supply base.

Given the new world that they are facing, OEMs should change their practices. Here are some suggestions:

Move beyond transactional behavior toward strategic partnerships

OEMs should recognize that a major benefit of having multiple suppliers is resiliency, and while competition between them will ensure fair pricing, it should not be used as a tool to drive a race to the bottom. Some firms already have a more enlightened view. For decades, Toyota has ensured that it understands a supplier's costs and then negotiates prices without repeated rounds of threats. It also works with individual suppliers to improve their productivity and performance. "You can sit and have conversations. They actually care," the CEO of one company told me. "I don't have the potential to make as much money [with them], but the business is really solid, very stable."

Large companies should also directly manage relationships with lower-tier suppliers that are strategically important.

Implement greater pricing flexibility in contracts

This means recognizing the reality that we are moving into an era of increased volatility in commodity and energy pricing. Approaches might include some form of indexing to commodity prices or frequent market pricing comparisons. If your first knowledge of one of your supplier's difficulties comes from a force majeure declaration or a notice of commercial impracticality, you have failed. If your supplier fails, it will only increase your costs as you have to seek alternatives under pressure.

Rethink inventory levels and where stock is carried

It is premature to proclaim the complete end of JIT inventory practices given that there still are many benefits to keeping low inventory in the pipeline that may be subject to engineering changes or at risk of being unneeded or becoming obsolete. But you should agree who in the supply chain should hold how much and who should assume the associated costs and risks. Detroit OEMs historically have used punitive contract penalties for supply shortfalls, and suppliers probably haven't sufficiently priced these risks into the contracts they signed. It's time for a more collaborative approach.

If we have learned anything about supply chains over the last few years, it is the need to adapt to new circumstances. It's time to take a more strategic view of supplier relationships. Manufacturers should remember the reason they outsourced in the first place was because the supplier did work that they themselves couldn't or didn't want to do internally. Healthy suppliers are a big part of a more resilient supply chain—one that can adapt in this rapidly changing world.

TAKEAWAYS

Many large original equipment manufacturers (OEMs) have long been ruthless with their suppliers, demanding extremely low prices and loading them up with risks. Given that the current turmoil buffeting global supply chains is unlikely to end anytime soon, OEMs should reconsider their supplier policies by doing the following:

✓ **Move beyond transactional behavior and treat suppliers more like partners.** Ensure that you understand your supplier's costs and negotiate without threats.

✓ **Implement greater price flexibility in contracts.** Approaches might include some form of indexing to commodity prices or frequent market pricing comparisons.

✓ **Rethink inventory levels and where in the supply chain stock is carried.** Take a more collaborative approach by agreeing who in the supply chain should hold how much inventory and who should assume the associated costs and risks.

NOTE

1. Vince Bond Jr., "Stellantis: Suppliers Bear All the Risk," *Automotive News*, February 4, 2022, https://www.autonews.com/suppliers/stellantis-shifts-risk-suppliers.

Adapted from content posted on hbr.org, April 6, 2022 (product #H06Z1S).

10

DIGITAL TRANSFORMATION IS CHANGING SUPPLY CHAIN RELATIONSHIPS

by Maria Jesús Saénz, Elena Revilla, and Inma Borrella

The digital transformation of businesses is creating new products, processes, and services. But to provide these new offerings, companies must share information and assets with each other in ways that were previously off-limits. For example, digitized services may require competitors to share physical assets such as warehouse space.

This, in turn, means that companies will need to change the way they forge and manage relationships with other entities in the supply chain to facilitate new types of alliances and agreements. It will require managers responsible for developing supply chain relationships, such as account managers or supply managers, to adopt a *boundary-spanning mindset* in order to facilitate collaboration, experimentation, and trust across organizational boundaries.

Offerings That Are Redefining Relationships

One supply chain process that requires such interactions is collaborative forecasting informed by machine-learning-based algorithms, which use real-time information on buying patterns to identify new parameters that affect demand. To fully exploit these insights, companies need deeper interactions with upstream suppliers and customers downstream.

Or consider a product that is redrawing supply chain relationships: a smart infant pacifier that gathers information on children's health, such as body temperatures and medications. Manufacturers of the product, their suppliers, and retailers can use these new streams of data to refine the product and create new ones. Doing so, however, requires them to establish more expansive collaborative relationships. For example, retailers could give customers free registrations to an app that monitors the pacifier's usage. The manufacturer and suppliers could use this data to develop customized accessories based on how the product is used.

Examples of services that would necessitate new relationships are digital tools and platforms that enhance a supply chain's agility and flexibility by enabling companies to switch from asset ownership to asset sharing. They provide a good illustration of how digital transformation changes the dynamics of interactions between companies.

Consider on-demand warehousing from providers such as Flexe. These services identify unused industrial storage space and make it available to companies on a short-term basis. Sharing the space in this way enables the owner of the space to defray the cost of its unproductive asset and better align its warehousing needs with others' demands. It allows the service buyer to meet its changing storage requirements without having to add an expensive asset to its portfolio. However, the owner might have to accept that companies interested in sharing its warehouse facility may be archrivals—an accommodation that was difficult to justify before digital transformation opened the door to this type of service.

Then there is the Walmart GoLocal platform, which allows other retailers, restaurants, or online services, small and large, to use Walmart's own delivery platform to complete last-mile deliveries to other merchants' customers. Platform users gain access to the retailer's transportation network as well as external gig drivers. Enterprises on the platform can leverage the diverse ecosystem of users to achieve new efficiencies. For instance, with so many delivery routes on the platform, there may be opportunities to share vehicle space on routes used by multiple companies. Pooling goods in this way improves vehicle utilization and lowers the cost of transportation.

As these examples show, companies have to be more open-minded about commercial rivalries if digital-transformation-driven asset-sharing services are to fulfill their potential.

Developing Boundary-Spanning Managers

The managers responsible for crafting and implementing these new relationships have to be open to unfamiliar ways of doing business. They must be able to identify the value of nontraditional opportunities, find the most appropriate partners, and create agreements that maximize the value captured while minimizing the potential risks. This means that companies that are digitizing their supply chains or planning to do so need to promote new roles and supporting systems. Here are some examples of these new approaches.

Identify collaboration opportunities

Managers need to encourage the exploration of other ways to leverage new relationships. For example, savvy digital companies should continuously test new technologies and develop prototypes with partners and their customers. Walmart is experimenting with using live-streaming technology in collaboration with TikTok to offer customers new shopping experiences.

Create KPIs that reflect the gains from collaboration

Managers may need to expand the range of key performance indicators (KPIs) they use to encompass the opportunities created by digitization. For example, in addition to tracking established indicators such as on-time delivery, Walmart's GoLocal service measures gains from the delivery pooling arrangements that were not available to enterprises before joining the platform. Also, measurements like these provide evidence of quick wins and promote the scalability of benefits from digital initiatives.

Develop responsive contracts

Digitalization, and the communities of users it creates, can enable companies to develop contract systems that rapidly realign agreement terms with new business demands. For instance, Flex Pulse, a cloud-based platform built by global contract manufacturer Flex to give the company visibility into its manufacturing operations worldwide, also supports a digital contracts system. The system stores and manages contracts digitally and monitors operations involving Flex, its suppliers, and its customers in real time. Contractual terms such as incentives can be altered quickly in response to shifting market conditions. Also, the system uses AI algorithms to track supplier performance and identify opportunities to improve the efficiency of joint operations. These opportunities can be speedily translated into revised contractual terms.

Boundary spanners will become essential change agents in the new era that digital transformation is making possible. Without them, companies will struggle to compete in the new world.

TAKEAWAYS

Digital technologies are allowing companies to share supply chain information and assets in new ways. These new opportunities will require managers to become boundary spanners—facilitating collaboration, experimentation, and trust across organizational boundaries. They can do so in three ways:

✓ **Identify collaboration opportunities.** Explore different ways to leverage new relationships, such as testing new technologies and developing prototypes with partners and their customers.

✓ **Expand the range of KPIs to include opportunities created by digitization.** Doing so can provide evidence of quick wins and promote the scalability of benefits from digital initiatives.

✓ **Develop responsive contract systems.** Digitalization can enable companies to develop contract systems that rapidly realign agreement terms with new business demands.

Adapted from content posted on hbr.org, July 7, 2022 (product #H0744L).

11

HOW WALMART AUTOMATED SUPPLIER NEGOTIATIONS

by Remko Van Hoek, Michael DeWitt,
Mary Lacity, and Travis Johnson

Walmart, like most organizations with large procurement operations, has challenges conducting focused negotiations with all of its 100,000-plus suppliers. As a result, around 20% of its suppliers have signed agreements with cookie-cutter terms that are often not negotiated. It's not the optimal way to engage with these "tail-end suppliers"—for the company or its suppliers.

But the cost of hiring more human buyers to negotiate with them would exceed any additional value.

Walmart solved the problem with artificial intelligence (AI)–powered software that includes a text-based interface (or chatbot) that negotiates with human suppliers on behalf of Walmart. Walmart Canada piloted the solution in January 2021 and used supplier feedback to hone the system. Walmart has since deployed the solution in three other countries, and Walmart operations in more countries plan to implement the technology soon.

Here, we share four lessons on how to use automated procurement negotiations in ways that benefit both buyers and suppliers. Such systems can generate savings, improve the terms for both parties, and increase the flexibility and resiliency of a supply chain.

The Pilot

With advances in AI, Walmart began exploring the possibility of automating procurement negotiations for tail-end suppliers and licensed a software product called Pactum AI in 2019. The deployment was postponed because of Covid-19, but one of us (Michael DeWitt) resurrected the initiative a year later, in January 2021, for his organization, Walmart International.

Since Walmart already had experimented with the software in a sandbox environment, Walmart International moved directly to a small pilot in the company's Canadian business. The pilot, which lasted three months, included a variety of stakeholders—89 suppliers, five buyers, and representatives from Walmart Canada's finance, treasury, and legal departments—and Pactum, the company that had created the underlying AI technology.

At the outset, Walmart International estimated that the system would yield a positive return on investment if the chatbot could close deals with 20% of the suppliers involved in the pilot. The retailer selected "goods not for resale"—categories such as fleet services, carts, and other equipment used in retail stores—and not products sold to Walmart customers. It decided to focus on suppliers for whom there was accurate data on payment terms and where there was clear opportunity to improve payment terms and secure additional discounts.

Walmart International targeted payment schedules, hoping to negotiate early payment discounts or extended payment terms without discounts. In exchange, Walmart would offer suppliers the option to change Walmart's right to terminate contracts immediately without cause (known as "termination for convenience") to providing a 30-, 60-, or 90-day written termination notice. Walmart would also selectively offer suppliers opportunities for growth in assortment and sales volume in exchange for price discounts.

Internal buyers selected the suppliers to target and created training scenarios for Pactum AI's machine learning algorithm. The scenarios were used to create structured scripts to guide suppliers through negotiations. Suppliers could respond to scenarios at their own pace.

Walmart International invited around 100 tail-end suppliers to try the solution. Eighty-nine agreed to participate. The chatbot was successful in reaching an agreement with 64% of them—well above the 20% target—and with an average negotiation turnaround of 11 days.

In post-pilot interviews with suppliers that engaged in successful negotiations, 83% of them described the system as easy to use and liked the ability to make a counteroffer and the time the system gave them to think about the negotiation at their own pace. For example, Ben Garisto, president of MIWE, a bakery-equipment manufacturer, said, "During in-person negotiations, you do not always have the questions in advance, and you are responding in real time. Other types of automated requests for proposals sometimes feel a bit like a template with little room to tell your story."

Several suppliers, however, still would have liked to negotiate face-to-face. Other suppliers wanted a less verbose, more fluid script instead of prohibiting suppliers from backtracking to early steps in the negotiation.

During the production pilot, Walmart gained, on average, 1.5% in savings on the spend negotiated and an extension of payment terms to an average of 35 days. Walmart then improved the scenarios and scripts and extended the solution to suppliers in the United States, Chile, and South Africa. So far, the chatbot has closed deals with 68% of the suppliers approached and generated an average savings of 3%.

Lessons Learned

Other companies interested in automating procurement can apply these lessons on how to develop and introduce such a system.

1. Move to a production pilot quickly

The AI journey for many companies languishes in the proof-of-concept phase—fewer than half make it into production, according to Gartner.[1] That's because proof-of-concept phases focus on technical capabilities instead of business goals. Walmart decided to skip a proof-of-concept phase and to go straight to a production pilot focused on business goals.

Walmart's "business owners"—people in charge of budgets and responsible for the spend with suppliers (for example, operations for store supplies and IT for hardware and software)—helped to create negotiation use cases and scenarios. Walmart's buyers provided crucial subject-matter expertise on the negotiation scenarios needed to train the chatbot and nominated suppliers to participate in the pilot (based on which suppliers conduct enough business with Walmart to warrant a negotiation and which would welcome a chance to negotiate). The legal team made sure the chatbot's script and resulting contract conformed to Walmart contracting standards and policy.

2. Start with indirect-spend categories and preapproved suppliers

Walmart began with goods not for resale to minimize the risks to the business posed by the testing of a new procurement practice. Walmart also focused on preapproved suppliers so the need to validate new suppliers wouldn't delay the start of the pilot.

3. Decide on acceptable trade-offs

Automated procurement requires precisely defining the boundaries of what the buyer is willing to concede in exchange for what it wants. For example, the AI chatbot needs to know the specific trade-offs the buyer is willing to give for, say, moving from full payments in 10 days after receipt of the invoice to receiving payment 15, 20, 30, 45, or 60 days after receipt of invoice in exchange for improved termination terms and the opportunities for suppliers to expand their business with Walmart.

4. Scale by extending geographies, categories, and use cases

Walmart's motto for this project was to "nail it and scale it." Successful production pilots helped Walmart sell the solution to other parts of the business. After the pilot in Canada, the United States, Chile, and South Africa, deployments in Walmart's other markets are imminent. The categories have also expanded to include route rate negotiations for transportation and some goods for resale. Some mid-tier suppliers now use the system, and the chatbot is multilingual.

Scaling has increased productivity because the software learns from every negotiation, reducing the setup time for new categories. Additionally, the chatbot can run 2,000 negotiations simultaneously—something no human buyer can do.

One can see the trajectory: As terms and conditions become more algorithmic, fewer suppliers and parts of spend pools will go unmanaged. Procurement professionals will focus less on negotiating agreements and more on strategic relationships, exceptions, and continuous improvement—benefiting both the buyer and suppliers.

TAKEAWAYS

It's an age-old problem in procurement: Corporate buyers lack the time to negotiate fully with all suppliers, which has left untapped value on the table for both buyers and suppliers. To address this challenge, Walmart deployed AI-powered negotiations software with a text-based interface—a chatbot—connect with suppliers.

✓ During the production pilot, Walmart gained, on average, 1.5% in savings on the spend negotiated and an extension of payment terms to an average of 35 days.

✓ So far, the chatbot is negotiating and closing agreements with 68% of suppliers approached, with each side gaining something it values.

✓ Successful pilots helped Walmart sell the solution to other parts of the business, and categories have expanded to include route rate negotiations and goods for resale.

✓ To deliver results from automated procurement negotiations: Move quickly to a production pilot, start with indirect-spend categories with preapproved suppliers, decide on acceptable trade-offs, and scale by extending geographies, categories, and use cases.

NOTE

1. John McCormick, "AI Project Failure Rates Near 50%, But It Doesn't Have to Be That Way, Say Experts," *Wall Street Journal*, August 7, 2020, https://www.wsj.com/articles/ai-project-failure -rates-near-50-but-it-doesnt-have-to-be-that-way-say-experts -11596810601.

Adapted from content posted on hbr.org, November 8, 2022 (product #H07CGI).

Section 5

IMPLEMENTING SUSTAINABLE PRACTICES

12

CONSUMER PRESSURE IS KEY TO FIXING DIRE LABOR CONDITIONS

by Robert Handfield, Tim Kraft, and Marguerite Moore

D espite decades of efforts and numerous initiatives to improve labor practices in apparel supply chains, worker rights violations continue to be rampant in low-cost countries. Increasing pressure from advocacy groups, financial analysts, and the media to address such incidents has led Western brands, NGOs, and third-party certification bodies to develop a plethora of diverse auditing programs that vary in terms of goals, scope, and commitment.

However, the potpourri of assessments (certifications, third-party audits, brand audits, and self-assessment audits) remain ineffective, and in fact conditions in many factories appear to be getting worse.[1] Audits and assessments are difficult for factory owners to navigate and have contributed to the high levels of audit fatigue seen throughout the industry. In our interviews with factory owners, we discovered that Tier 1 facilities dedicate extensive resources and personnel to ensure that they pass the variety of audits they are subject to throughout the year. But somehow, these audits are not curtailing many of the fundamental human rights violations in extended apparel supply networks.

The complexity behind social compliance assessments needs to be reduced. To that end, our multidisciplinary research team at North Carolina State University is developing a simplified system—which we call the Ethical Apparel Index (EAI)—to demystify the vast amount of audit data being collected and enhance transparency in the apparel industry. The essential framework for this index has been developed, and we are preparing to conduct a pilot test through a partnership with a variety of brands, retailers, and factory owners across the globe.

Today, the outcomes of apparel-factory audits are invisible to consumers, yet we know that many consumer segments, especially younger consumers, are eager to support producers who respect human rights in apparel production. This means that brands that mandate human rights compliance in factories throughout their supply chains are not getting rewarded in the marketplace. To remedy this problem, we developed a highly structured coding process that synthesizes the multitude of audit outcomes into a simplified message that can then easily be communicated to consumers.

Our goal is to make it possible for a consumer who is considering whether to buy a garment to scan a QR code that would take them to a simple, easy-to-understand summary of the ethical production performance of the factory that made the garment. This summary would let consumers know that they can trust that the brand is doing its best to improve its suppliers' factory conditions. It is our belief that this type of "market pull" mechanism will be far more effective than regulatory compliance "push" mechanisms in driving change in apparel supply chains. In doing so, we seek to create an independent source of truth based on the best available information that already exists; it would simplify the data produced by a plethora of methods for assessing factories that manufacture garments sold in retail channels.

Our research team is guided by an advisory board that includes stakeholders from all parts of the apparel supply chain, including WRAP, one of the largest third-party apparel-factory-certifications programs in the world; the American Apparel and Footwear Association; and Shahi, one of the largest apparel-factory groups in India. The Templeton World Charity Foundation is funding the effort.

Simplifying a Complex System of Audits

To improve transparency for consumers, we employed two rules of thumb that guided our goal of connecting consumers with the complex world of factory social compliance.

Let's agree that there is no perfect standard

There is no single standard that will meet the unique needs of brand audit. Audits are flawed by design—they are infrequent snapshots that can be gamed by suppliers and that rely on the judgment of auditors. However, the creation of a simplified score can provide evidence that a company is making a genuine effort and is following a set of established standards that most people would agree is sufficient.

Since supply chains are complex, let's start with Tier 1 suppliers

Auditing all suppliers in the network would be a large undertaking at the outset. We should start by ensuring that brands are driving the right behaviors within their Tier 1 suppliers—that is, the suppliers over which they have direct influence. In apparel, this is typically the "cut and sew" supplier that assembles the garment from various components. Later, lower tiers of suppliers (spinning mills, dye mills, and cotton farms) should be included.

We then addressed three broad questions:

1. What content should be included?

2. How could this content be effectively communicated to consumers?

3. How could the credibility of EAI data be ensured?

In deciding what content to include, we recognized early on in our work that to communicate effectively to apparel consumers, the confusing array of different audit standards must be simplified. Our goal is not to replace the audit standards being used but instead to take advantage of the fact that there is significant overlap across standards to produce a simplified summary of ethical production performance of factories that can then be easily communicated to consumers.

Accordingly, we developed a taxonomy based on an analysis of 10 sets of labor standards developed by organizations such as the UN's International Labor Board, governments, and NGOs and about 30 different audit systems used in third-party certification programs. We then synthesized it into eight common themes concerning essential working conditions in factories: nondiscrimination, no harassment and abuse, no forced labor, no child labor, freedom of association, health and safety, humane working hours, and fair compensation (see table 12-1, "Reducing the eight common themes in standards and audits to three simple questions").

Based on our interviews with supply chain stakeholders, we reduced the eight categories to three key questions. The answers to those questions can provide consumers with enough information to understand the working conditions inside an apparel factory without overloading them:

- Are the workers treated fairly in the workplace?

- Are the workers working in a safe environment?

- Are the workers paid fairly?

TABLE 12-1

Reducing the eight common themes in standards and audits to three simple questions

Labor standards and questions used in most audits of apparel factories' labor practices can be grouped into eight common themes. The information related to the themes can then be used to answer three simple questions, which can provide consumers with visibility into the working conditions at the factories that make the apparel they are considering purchasing.

Common themes	Questions designed to provide consumers with easy-to-digest information
Nondiscrimination: Ensuring the appropriate treatment of workers, especially women and minorities	Are the workers treated fairly in the workplace?
Harassment and abuse: Preventing worker harassment and bullying and providing programs to prevent it in the workplace	
Forced labor: Prohibiting illegal actions such as restrictions on movement from one's place of work, threatening income withholding, and forced overtime	
Child labor: Complying with the country's minimum-age policy, as well as having policies and providing documentation for young workers	
Freedom of association: Ensuring workers' rights to organize and form collective bargaining associations	
Health and safety: Complying with regulatory requirements for all aspects of facility safety, including access to bathrooms, dormitories, canteens, and first aid	Are the workers working in a safe environment?
Working hours: Providing payroll documentation that verifies compliance with legal working hours and the payment of overtime rates	Are the workers paid fairly?
Compensation: Complying with minimum wage, equal remuneration, leave with pay, and other compensation requirements	

Note: Ethical Apparel Index project team's analysis of 12 sets of labor standards and 27 third-party certification programs developed by organizations such as the UN's International Labour Board, governments, and NGOs and approximately 30 different audit systems used in third-party certification programs.

A Call to Action for Brands

The EAI will only be as good as the audit data upon which it is built, and there is much work ahead to improve the system of audits and assessments that form the basis for the EAI. Our research suggests that brands should consider using a recognized independent third party such as WRAP or SA8000 to conduct audits and certify factories rather than relying on their own internal auditors. Third parties are moving to more standardized audit frameworks that can provide objective audit data that serves as an input to the EAI.

Employing unbiased third parties would not only make it possible for a single audit of a factory to be conducted for multiple brands but also send a message to consumers that "the fox is not guarding the henhouse"—that is, would be more credible than the results produced by brands' own auditors. To enhance our database of supplier audits and further strengthen the EAI, we are working with partner companies to augment the EAI with crowdsourced data such as texts and phone-app survey responses from factory workers.

Admittedly, our approach poses a risk to the thousands of parties: brands, factories, and distributors. What if a factory audit reveals a problem that is then exposed to consumers? But whether they like it or not, transparency is rapidly becoming an expectation in retail markets. It may be time for brands to admit to consumers that their supply chain has some problems but that they are doing their best to make factories a safe and fair place for workers.

TAKEAWAYS

Different audit systems and standards for assessing labor practices in the apparel supply chain remain ineffective in improving working conditions. But a new system in development would synthesize the multitude of audit outcomes into a simplified score that can then easily be communicated to consumers.

✓ There is no perfect standard that will meet the unique needs of a brand audit, but the creation of a simplified score can provide evidence of whether a company is making a genuine effort.

✓ Start with Tier 1 suppliers, then move on to others in the network.

✓ Aim to answer three key questions: (1) Are the workers treated fairly in the workplace? (2) Are the workers working in a safe environment? (3) Are the workers paid fairly?

✓ By following this approach, a company could harness the voice of the consumer and offer transparency in the effort to improve labor practices.

NOTE

1. Sofia Nazalya, "Worldwide Decline in Labour Rights Strikes at Heart of Global Supply Chains," Verisk Maplecroft, October 6, 2021, https://www.maplecroft.com/insights/analysis/worldwide-decline-in-labour-rights-strikes-at-heart-of-global-supply-chains/.

Adapted from "Consumer Pressure Is Key to Fixing Dire Labor Conditions in the Clothing Supply Chain," on hbr.org, November 2, 2022 (product #H07BMP).

13

A MORE SUSTAINABLE SUPPLY CHAIN

by Verónica H. Villena and Dennis A. Gioia

In recent years a rising number of multinational corporations (MCNs) have pledged to work only with suppliers that adhere to social and environmental standards. Typically, these MNCs expect their first-tier suppliers to comply with those standards, and they ask that those suppliers in turn ask for compliance from *their* suppliers—who ideally ask the same from *their* suppliers. And so on. The aim is to create a cascade of sustainable practices that flows smoothly throughout the supply chain, or, as we prefer to call it, the supply network.

It's an admirable idea, but it's been hard to realize in practice. Many of the MNCs that have committed to it have faced scandals brought about by suppliers that, despite being aware of sustainability standards, have nevertheless gone on to violate them. Consider the embarrassing scrutiny that Apple, Dell, and HP endured not long ago for sourcing electronics from overseas companies that required employees to work in hazardous conditions, and the fallout that Nike and Adidas suffered for using suppliers that were dumping toxins into rivers in China.

What's more, all those scandals involved first-tier suppliers. The practices of lower-tier suppliers are almost always worse, increasing companies' exposure to serious financial, social, and environmental risks. In this article we describe various ways that MNCs can defuse the ticking time bomb those risks represent.

Where the Problems Are

To understand the situation and develop ideas for tackling it, we conducted a study of three supply networks. Each was headed by an MNC considered to be a "sustainability leader"—one in the automotive industry, one in electronics, and one in pharmaceuticals and consumer products. We also studied a representative set of each MNC's suppliers—a total of nine top-tier and 22 lower-tier suppliers, based variously in Mexico, China, Taiwan, and the United States. What we discovered was that many were violating the standards that the MNCs expected them to adhere to. The hoped-for cascade effect was seldom occurring.

We found problems in every country we studied. In Mexico we visited five lower-tier suppliers; all lacked environmental management systems, and four lacked procedures for handling red-flag social problems such as sexual harassment, retaliation by supervisors, and hazardous labor conditions. At three of the companies, temporary workers made up nearly 50% of the workforce, and turnover rates sometimes reached 100%, making it difficult to implement viable environmental, health, and safety programs. In China and Taiwan, we visited 10 lower-tier suppliers, all of which had marginal environmental practices, dangerous working conditions, and chronic overtime issues. In the United States we studied seven lower-tier suppliers and found that three had high concentrations of airborne chemicals and a lack of systematic accident reporting.

The pattern is worrisome. Remember, all those suppliers were connected to model firms that were working proactively to encourage sustainability. If exemplary MNCs are having trouble ensuring good practices among their lower-tier suppliers, then "regular" firms, in all likelihood, are faring even worse at this.

The problem, ironically, often starts with the MNCs themselves. They frequently place orders that exceed suppliers' capacity or impose unrealistic deadlines, leading supplier factories to demand heavy overtime from their workers. When we asked a representative at one supplier why his company had violated a 60-hour workweek limit, he gave us a frank explanation: "We didn't want to tell our customer that we can't produce its products on time, because otherwise it's going to try to find someone else that can. But our customer didn't give us enough notice to hire enough skilled people to do the job."

First-tier suppliers, for their part, rarely concern themselves with their own suppliers' sustainability practices. That's often because they're struggling with sustainability issues themselves. The noncompliant company we cited above, for example, doesn't try to enforce a strict 60-hour workweek limit with any of its suppliers. "We don't comply with this requirement ourselves," the representative told us, "so how could we ask our own suppliers to do so?"

For MNCs, there are special challenges in governing lower-tier suppliers. There's often no direct contractual relationship, and a particular MNC's business often doesn't mean that much to the lower-tier supplier. If American and Japanese automakers rely heavily on a certain seat maker, for example, they can demand that it adhere to their sustainability standards. But that seat maker may have a hard time getting *its* suppliers to follow suit. Suppose it does business with a foam manufacturer that has many other big customers in the electronics, appliance, and health care industries—each of which has different sustainability standards. The foam manufacturer has little incentive to conform to the automakers' sustainability requirements, because the automakers account for only a small fraction of its total business.

Furthermore, most lower-tier suppliers are not well known, so they receive relatively little attention and pressure from the media, NGOs, and other stakeholders. Even when they do attract attention (for sexual harassment problems, for example, or chronic overtime demands), we found that they do not feel the need to address the issues involved. They tend to act only when MNCs intervene.

Lower-tier suppliers are also the least equipped to handle sustainability requirements. They often do not have sustainability expertise or resources, and they may be unaware of accepted social and environmental practices and regulations. They are also frequently located in countries where such regulations are nonexistent, lax, or not enforced at all. And typically, they don't know much about the sustainability requirements imposed by MNCs—but even if they do, they have no incentive to comply. This may explain why most of the lower-tier suppliers in our study lacked programs to dispose of toxic waste and in fact had no environmental management program whatsoever.

MNCs, too, are handicapped by ignorance. They frequently don't even know who their lower-tier suppliers are, let alone where they're located or what capabilities they have (or don't have). Many of the 22 lower-tier suppliers in our study are small or medium-size private firms that provide little information to the public—characteristics that, in effect, make them almost invisible. Several directors of the three MNCs we studied viewed this as a big problem. "The demon in this place," one of them said, "is the [lower-tier] suppliers that I know the least about." Another said, "I don't have control over the ones that pose the highest risks, so I'm losing sleep over them."

All these concerns mean that lower-tier suppliers are unquestionably the riskiest members of a supply network.

If they have poor or dubious sustainability performance, then an MNC that does business with them can endanger its reputation and suffer profound repercussions—losing customers, being forced to find new suppliers, or having its supply chain disrupted. To reduce such risks, MNCs need to include both first-tier and lower-tier suppliers in their sustainability programs.

Best Practices

The three MNCs in our study have taken a number of steps to promote suppliers' social and environmental responsibility:

- They have established long-term sustainability goals.

- They require first-tier suppliers to set their own long-term sustainability goals.

- They include lower-tier suppliers in the overall sustainability strategy.

- They task a point person on staff with extending the firm's sustainability program to first- and lower-tier suppliers.

These are all beneficial measures that other companies should consider adopting. Firms can also borrow some of the specific strategies that our MNCs use to spread good practices throughout their supply networks. These fall into four broad categories:

Direct approach

The MNCs we studied set and monitor social and environmental targets for their first-tier suppliers regarding second-tier suppliers. The automotive corporation, for instance, has a strong commitment to supplier diversity. It requires its first-tier suppliers to allocate 7% of their procurement spending to minority suppliers. Some first-tier suppliers were already meeting that target; others have made substantial changes to do so (for example, by changing performance criteria for their purchasing managers). The first-tier suppliers we interviewed noted that the MNC periodically checks to see if the target is being met and creates opportunities to help them network with minority lower-tier suppliers.

Another MNC annually surveys its first-tier suppliers to gather information not only about their health, safety, labor, and environmental practices but also about the sustainability performance of their lower-tier suppliers. The surveys seem to be having the desired effect: They've prompted first-tier suppliers to engage in internal discussions about whether they should and could alter their procurement practices (to adopt industrywide sustainability standards, for example). And on two occasions, firms have made changes to comply with MNC requirements (such as using key performance indicators to monitor supplier sustainability).

Additionally, the three MNCs work with their major suppliers to map the connections and interdependencies in their supply networks, including those at the lower-tier level. This allows them to identify potentially risky lower-tier suppliers and to work with the major suppliers to deploy customized risk-mitigation programs where needed.

Indirect approach

The MNCs we studied delegate elements of lower-tier-supplier sustainability management to their first-tier suppliers. This approach is effective because the MNCs are hands-on: They offer training to suppliers and provide some incentives for implementing sustainability practices. Most of the first-tier suppliers we interviewed told us that such training had led them to make substantial changes in their manufacturing processes and to begin asking *their* suppliers to adopt similar sustainability standards.

Managing Lower-Tier Supplier Sustainability

Ideally, multinational corporations will use a combination of approaches—direct, indirect, collective, and global—to encourage sustainable practices throughout their supply networks. Some specific strategies within each type of approach are listed below.

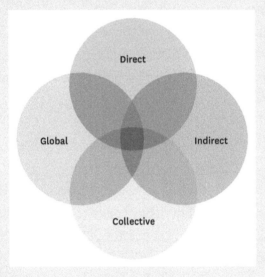

Direct

- Evaluate first-tier suppliers by using sustainability performance indicators that capture their requirements for lower-tier suppliers.

- Survey suppliers on their environmental, health, safety, and labor practices and on their procurement practices.

- Work with major first-tier suppliers to map the firm's supply network.

Indirect

- Provide training and foster peer learning among first-tier suppliers to help them improve their procurement practices with lower-tier suppliers.

- Select high-performing suppliers to pilot new sustainability initiatives.

- Reward suppliers for cascading sustainability requirements to lower-tier suppliers.

Collective

- Commit to developing and complying with industrywide sustainability standards, and help suppliers become full members of industry organizations.

- Via industry organizations, share resources with competitors and major suppliers to achieve sustainability goals.

(continued)

Managing Lower-Tier Supplier Sustainability

- Encourage first- and lower-tier suppliers to take advantage of sustainability training programs offered by industry organizations.

Global

- Work closely with relevant NGOs and international institutions interested in improving supply chain sustainability.

- Use tools and data that those organizations provide for dealing with suppliers (contracts and scorecards).

- Recognize suppliers that excel in programs sponsored by NGOs and international institutions.

The three MNCs have also created preferred-supplier programs aimed at fostering peer learning about sustainability. One corporation, for instance, invites its most socially and environmentally responsible suppliers to join an exclusive group that enables them to strengthen relationships with the MNC and exchange best sustainability practices with one another. Several of these suppliers have started to set their own sustainability requirements for the suppliers they use.

To further encourage first-tier suppliers to cascade the MNCs' sustainability requirements into their own supply networks, MNCs can use supplier sustainability awards, long-term contracts, and preferred status.

Collective approach

Our MNCs collaborate with their competitors and major suppliers to develop and disseminate industrywide sustainability standards. They recognize that a single MNC cannot be expected to fight alone against the problematic labor or environmental practices of global suppliers. Doing so would be not only prohibitively expensive but also unfair, because in most sectors, the major corporations use many of the same suppliers.

The MNCs we studied are all founding members of industry associations focused on developing sustainability standards, providing assessment tools, and offering training to first- and lower-tier suppliers. One notable association is the Responsible Business Alliance (RBA), whose members include Intel, HP, IBM, Dell, Philips, and Apple.

Collaborative initiatives have many benefits. They can increase efficiencies for suppliers, who can use a standardized self-assessment or audit to satisfy many customers and thus avoid duplication. These initiatives can also draw in more suppliers, because suppliers that have many customers with the same sustainability requirements tend to be more willing to participate. And collaboration can make sustainability initiatives more feasible, because industrywide training is subsidized by members.

Additionally, when MNCs help their first-tier suppliers become full members of an industry association, those suppliers must then comply with industry standards, which means they have to assess their own suppliers' sustainability. The RBA, for example, requires its full members to conduct approved audits annually for at least 25% of their own high-risk facilities *and* 25% of their high-risk suppliers' facilities. (Risk here is assessed along labor, health and safety, environmental, and ethical dimensions.)

Industry associations have a unique power over both first- and lower-tier suppliers, as most of their members are major players in their sectors. Consider the electronics maker Flex, a full member of the RBA and a first-tier supplier for many MNCs. A second-tier electronics supplier is unlikely to refuse a request from Flex for a compliance audit, because it knows that Flex itself has passed this audit and that most other top-tier electronics suppliers, to stay competitive, will probably start issuing similar audit requests.

Global approach

The MNCs we studied make a point of collaborating with international organizations and NGOs that share their goals. For instance, all three corporations have joined the United Nations Global Compact, an international effort to promote corporate social responsibility. The three MNCs also participate in the Carbon Disclosure Project's (CDP's) Supply Chain Program, a global data-collection platform in which suppliers disclose information about their carbon emissions. Firms such as Microsoft, Johnson & Johnson, and Walmart use this platform to engage their suppliers in being transparent about their environmental impact. Several participating suppliers told us that as a result, they are now collecting previously unsolicited information and making investments to try to reduce their carbon footprints.

The progress is encouraging: According to the CDP's 2019 supply chain report, 35% of the program members engaged with their suppliers on climate change in 2018, up from 23% the year before. Additionally, the report noted, "as suppliers become more mature in their understanding of sustainability issues and advance their approaches for taking action, there is evidence that they too are improving in their efforts to cascade positive change downwards through their own supply chains." This is occurring not only because MNCs have asked their suppliers to disclose their carbon emissions but also because that information influences how the MNCs contract with suppliers. One of the corporations we studied has created an award to recognize the suppliers that have improved the most in terms of CDP Supply Chain Program performance. Another MNC includes the program's ratings in its supplier scorecard and monitors those ratings annually.

Room for Improvement

The MNCs in our study have successfully addressed some of the problematic sustainability practices of their suppliers. But as we've already noted, there's plenty of room for improvement in what they're doing. In our research, we identified a few critical shortcomings in their operations when it comes to developing sustainability beyond first-tier suppliers.

First, the MNCs' engineering and procurement units often preapprove lower-tier suppliers, but their vetting criteria don't include social and environmental considerations. In other words, engineering and procurement address only the first of the proverbial three Ps of sustainability (profit), focusing on such issues as cost, quality, delivery, and technology, while overlooking the second and third Ps (people and the planet). Not surprisingly, that can lead to situations in which preapproved lower-tier suppliers violate the sustainability requirements of the MNCs they work with. The first-tier suppliers are then in a tough spot. Like it or not, they have to work with preapproved suppliers—but they are held accountable if those companies mistreat workers or harm the environment. As one exasperated manager said while describing this conundrum, "I am just using the supplier you asked me to use!"

Such predicaments are not uncommon. Different functional units of an MNC (engineering, procurement, sustainability) may pursue different agendas in interacting with first- and lower-tier suppliers—with results that do systemic damage to the corporation's overall sustainability effort and undermine its credibility. To avoid this, MNCs should set convergent sustainability goals and align the incentives for *all* functions that interact with first- and lower-tier suppliers.

A second problem is lack of sustainability training and incentives for procurement officers. All of the 52 procurement employees we interviewed (at MNCs and at suppliers) said they needed more training to properly pursue supplier sustainability on behalf of their firms. Arguably, they need more incentives as well: Companies must reward them for hitting all three Ps—that is, not just cost, quality, and delivery goals but also social and environmental ones. Our research suggests that isn't yet happening in a meaningful way. For the procurement professionals we interviewed, cost savings were unquestionably the top priority, followed by quality improvement and on-time delivery. Social and environmental concerns were notably absent. We should add that although companies at every level of the supply network need to provide more training and incentives for their procurement officers, supplier firms are likely to do so only if MNCs lead the way.

A third shortcoming we observed is that although our three MNCs devote considerable effort to developing their first-tier suppliers' sustainability capabilities, they have little direct contact with their first-tier suppliers' procurement personnel. As a result, those people are poorly informed about the MNCs' sustainability requirements and cannot communicate them clearly to their own suppliers, much less enforce them. To alleviate that problem, MNCs could invite suppliers' procurement personnel to their sustainability training sessions (along with environmental, health, and safety personnel) and encourage them to participate in industrywide sustainability training. Alternatively, MNCs could engage the top executives at their first-tier suppliers and explain the importance of building a sustainable supply network, with the goal of motivating them to catalyze the dissemination of sustainability requirements to lower-tier suppliers.

Conclusion

Many multinational corporations sincerely want to embed fair labor practices and environmental responsibility throughout their supply networks. A good way to start is by adopting the sustainability strategies used by the three MNCs in our study. But all corporations can and should do more. They should send their suppliers a more consistent message that economic, social, and environmental requirements are *all* important. They should make the same message clear to their procurement officials and create incentives for them to pursue not only economic goals but also environmental and social goals. Those officials should take a hands-on approach to collecting data about suppliers' capacity, monitoring indicators of their sustainability performance, and engaging with them in continuous improvement projects. The MNCs should also work directly with their suppliers' procurement units on the best ways to disseminate sustainability requirements throughout their supply networks. The danger of not acting is clear: A supply chain is only as strong as its weakest link.

TAKEAWAYS

Increasingly, multinational corporations (MNCs) are pledging to procure the materials and services they need from companies committed to fair labor practices and environmental protections. In reality, their suppliers—especially those at low levels of the chain—often violate sustainability standards.

✓ Leading companies in sustainability have established long-term sustainability goals. They try to cascade good practices all the way down to lower-tier suppliers, using a combination of direct, indirect, industrywide, and global strategies.

✓ All MNCs have more work to do to develop sustainable supply networks. They must emphasize

social and environmental responsibility, along
with economic considerations, at every level of the
supply chain; and they must give their procurement officers better training and incentives to pursue supplier sustainability.

✓ To encourage widespread dissemination of best
practices, they should be in direct contact with
the procurement officers at their first-tier suppliers. After all, a supply chain is only as strong as its
weakest link.

Adapted from Harvard Business Review, *March–April 2020 (product #R2002F).*

About the Contributors

STEVEN A. ALTMAN is a senior research scholar, adjunct assistant professor, and director of the DHL Initiative on Globalization at the NYU Stern Center for the Future of Management.

CAROLINE R. BASTIAN is a research scholar at the DHL Initiative on Globalization at the NYU Stern Center for the Future of Management.

INMA BORRELLA is a research scientist at the MIT Center for Transportation & Logistics. She is also the academic lead of the MITx MicroMasters in Supply Chain Management Program.

THOMAS Y. CHOI is a professor of supply chain management at Arizona State University's W. P. Carey School of Business. He is a codirector of the Complex Adaptive Supply Networks Research Accelerator (CASN-RA). He is the author of the forthcoming book *The Nature of Supply Networks*.

MICHAEL DEWITT is the vice president of strategic sourcing at Walmart International.

MIKE DOHERTY is a partner at Demand Clarity, where he specializes in helping retailers and their trading partners improve in-stocks and inventory performance. He is a coauthor (with André Martin and Jeff Harrop) of the book *Flowcasting the Retail Supply Chain.*

KASRA FERDOWS is the Heisley Family Professor of Global Manufacturing at Georgetown University's McDonough School of Business in Washington, DC.

SUKETU GANDHI is a cohead of the global Strategic Operations Practice at Kearney.

VISHAL GAUR is the Emerson Professor of Manufacturing Management and a professor of operations, technology, and information management at Cornell's SC Johnson College of Business.

DENNIS A. GIOIA is the Distinguished University Professor of Management, Emeritus, in the Smeal College of Business at Penn State University.

ROBERT HANDFIELD is the Bank of America Distinguished Professor of Operations and Supply Chain Management at North Carolina State University's Poole College of Management in Raleigh, North Carolina. He is a member of the Center for Advanced Purchasing's executive advisory board.

MORGANE HERCULANO is a research associate at Harvard Business School focusing on fintech and entrepreneurship. She graduated from Harvard College with a BA in economics, energy, and environment.

TRAVIS JOHNSON is the senior director of procurement enablement solutions at Walmart International.

TIM KRAFT is an associate professor of operations and supply chain management at North Carolina State University's Poole College of Management.

MARY LACITY is the David D. Glass Chair and a distinguished professor at the University of Arkansas's Sam M. Walton College of Business.

HAU L. LEE is the Thoma Professor of Operations, Information, and Technology at Stanford University's Graduate School of Business.

KAREN G. MILLS is a senior fellow at Harvard Business School and a leading authority on U.S. competitiveness, entrepreneurship, and innovation. She served in President Barack Obama's Cabinet as the administrator of the U.S. Small Business Administration (SBA) and was a member of the President's National Economic Council.

MARGUERITE MOORE is a professor at North Carolina State University's Wilson College of Textiles.

NIKOLAY OSADCHIY is an associate professor of information systems and operations management at Emory University's Goizueta Business School. He also is a senior editor at *Production and Operations Management.*

ELENA REVILLA is a professor and chair of the department of operations and technology management at IE Business School in Madrid. She is a postdoctoral fellow at the University of North Carolina at Chapel Hill and a visiting researcher at MIT.

ELISABETH B. REYNOLDS served as Special Assistant to the President for Manufacturing and Economic Development in the National Economic Council at the White House until October 2022. She is a lecturer in MIT's department of urban studies and planning and the former executive director of the MIT Task Force on the Work of the Future and the MIT Industrial Performance Center.

MARIA JESÚS SAÉNZ is the director of the Digital Supply Chain Transformation Lab at the MIT Center for Transportation and Logistics. She also serves as the executive director of the MIT supply chain management master's programs.

WOLFGANG SCHNELLBÄCHER is a partner and managing director based in BCG's Stuttgart office. He leads BCG's procurement activities in EMESA (Europe, Middle East, South America, and Africa). He is a coauthor of *Profit from the Source: Transforming Your Business by Putting Suppliers at the Core* and *Jumpstart to Digital Procurement*.

CHRISTIAN SCHUH is a senior partner and managing director based in BCG's Vienna office. He is a coauthor of *Profit from the Source: Transforming Your Business by Putting Suppliers at the Core* and *The Purchasing Chessboard*. He is a creator of the YouTube channel Procurement in the Park.

WILLY C. SHIH is the Robert and Jane Cizik Professor of Management Practice in Business Administration at Harvard Business School. He is a coauthor of *Producing Prosperity: Why America Needs a Manufacturing Renaissance* (Harvard Business Review Press, 2012).

MANMOHAN S. SODHI is a professor of operations and supply chain management at Bayes Business School in London.

He is a coauthor (with Navdeep S. Sodhi) of the *Harvard Business Review* article "Six Sigma Pricing" and (with Christopher S. Tang) of the book *Managing Supply Chain Risk*.

GEORGE STALK JR. is a senior partner (retired) of the Boston Consulting Group and a BCG fellow. He is the author of *Five Future Strategies You Need Right Now* (Harvard Business Review Press, 2008).

MAXIMILIANO UDENIO is an associate professor at the Research Centre for Operations Management at the Faculty of Economics and Business of the KU Leuven in Belgium.

REMKO VAN HOEK is a professor of supply chain management at the University of Arkansas's Sam M. Walton College of Business. He previously served as a chief procurement officer at a number of companies.

VERÓNICA H. VILLENA is an associate professor of supply chain management at W. P. Carey School of Business at Arizona State University.

DANIEL WEISE is a senior partner and managing director based in BCG's Düsseldorf office. He leads BCG's procurement activities globally. He is a coauthor of *Profit from* *the Source: Transforming Your Business by Putting Suppliers at the Core* and *Jumpstart to Digital Procurement.*

XIANDE ZHAO is the JD.com Chair Professor of Operations and Supply Chain Management at the China Europe International Business School.

Index

regional vs. global, xiv–xv
as webs/networks, 14–15
sustainability, xvi–xvii
best practices for, 143–152
cascading practices for, 137–157
collective approach for,
147–148, 149–151
consumer pressure and, 127–136
direct approach for, 144–145,
146–147
global approach for, 148,
151–152
improving, 152–155
indirect approach for, 145,
147
labor conditions and, 127–136
lower-tier suppliers and,
140–150, 153
managing lower-tier supplier,
146–148
problem areas around, 138–143

Taiwan Semiconductor Man-
ufacturing Corporation
(TSMC), 10, 81
Open Innovation Platform, 81
Taleb, Nassim Nicholas, 4
technology, xv. See also artificial
intelligence (AI)
digital transformation and,
107–113
for flow-casting, 73–74

just-in-time networks and,
27–28
regionalization and, 59
in risk assessment, 6–8
small/midsize suppliers and,
35, 36–37
in supplier negotiations,
115–123
in supply chain regionalization, 43–52
temporary workers, 139
Tesla, 11
3D printing. See additive
manufacturing
Tongyi Ceramics Science and
Technology, 81
Toyota, 21, 22–23, 24, 27
supplier relationships with,
102
trade-offs, 121
training, 36, 74, 154
transparency, 130–133, 135
transportation costs, 61
trust, xvi, 108

Udenio, Maximiliano, 13–19
Ukraine, war in, xii, 60–61,
62, 98
Unilever, 10
United Nations, 54, 132
Global Compact, 151
upskilling, 36

Is Your Business Ready for the Future?

If you enjoyed this book and want more on today's pressing business topics, turn to other books in the **Insights You Need** series from *Harvard Business Review*. Featuring HBR's latest thinking on topics critical to your company's success—from Blockchain and Cybersecurity to AI and Agile—each book will help you explore these trends and how they will impact you and your business in the future.

FOR MORE VISIT HBR.ORG/BOOKS

Harvard Business Review Press

The most important management ideas all in one place.

We hope you enjoyed this book from *Harvard Business Review*. Now you can get even more with HBR's 10 Must Reads Boxed Set. From books on leadership and strategy to managing yourself and others, this 6-book collection delivers articles on the most essential business topics to help you succeed.

HBR's 10 Must Reads Series

The definitive collection of ideas and best practices on our most sought-after topics from the best minds in business.

- Change Management
- Collaboration
- Communication
- Emotional Intelligence
- Innovation
- Leadership
- Making Smart Decisions

- Managing Across Cultures
- Managing People
- Managing Yourself
- Strategic Marketing
- Strategy
- Teams
- The Essentials

hbr.org/mustreads

Buy for your team, clients, or event.
Visit hbr.org/bulksales for quantity discount rates.